THE BIBLE
BOOK BY BOOK

THE BIBLE BOOK BY BOOK

*a fifty-two week study
of the sixty-six books of the Bible*

Roger Ellsworth

EVANGELICAL PRESS

EVANGELICAL PRESS
Faverdale North Industrial Estate, Darlington,
DL3 0PH, England

Evangelical Press USA
P. O. Box 84, Auburn, MA 01501, USA

e-mail: sales@evangelical-press.org
web: http://www.evangelicalpress.org

First published 2002

**British Library Cataloguing in Publication Data
available**

ISBN 0 85234 486 4

Printed and bound in Great Britain by Creative Print
and Design Wales, Ebbw Vale, South Wales.

*The following pages are affectionately dedicated
to the members of the Pastor's Class
of Immanuel Baptist Church*

CONTENTS

HOW TO USE *THE GUIDE*

The Bible book by book is the first book in a new series called *The Guide* and is a complete overview of all the books of the Bible. The series itself covers books of the Bible on an individual basis, such as *Colossians and Philemon*, and relevant topics such as *Christian comfort*. The series aim is to communicate the Christian faith in a straightforward and readable way.

Each book in *The Guide* will cover a book of the Bible or topic in some detail, but will be contained in relatively short and concise chapters. There will be questions at the end of each chapter for personal study or group discussion, to help you to study the Word of God more deeply.

An innovative and exciting feature of *The Guide* is that it is linked to its own web site. As well as being encouraged to search God's Word for yourself, you are invited to ask questions related to the book on the web site, where you will not only be able to have your own questions answered, but also be able to see a selection of answers that have been given to other readers. The web site can be found at www.evangelicalpress.org/TheGuide. Once you are on the site you just need to click on the 'select' button at the top of the page, according to the book on which you wish to post a question. Your question will then be answered either by Michael Bentley, the web site co-ordinator and

author of *Colossians and Philemon*, or others who have been selected because of their experience, their understanding of the Word of God and their dedication to working for the glory of the Lord.

There are two other books being published with *The Bible book by book*, on Colossians and Philemon, and Ecclesiastes, and many more will follow. It is the publisher's hope that you will be stirred to think more deeply about the Christian faith, and will be helped and encouraged in living out your Christian life, through the study of God's Word, in the difficult and demanding days in which we live.

POST-EXILIC TIMELINE

539	Babylon falls to Persia
	Cyrus issues the decree permitting Jews to return to homeland (Ezra 1:1-4)
536	First return of Jews under Zerubbabel (Ezra 1:5 - 2:70; Neh. 12)
	Total number of returnees — around 50,000 (Ezra 2:64-67)
536-535	Altar built at Jerusalem on site of temple
	— Feast of Tabernacles kept
	— Sacrifices observed
	— Foundations of temple laid (Ezra 3:7-13)
535-534	Opposition to the temple project from neighbouring Samaritans (Ezra 4:1-5)
534	Work on temple ceases (Ezra 4:24)
536-520	Israel's ruler is Zerubbabel who represents the king of Persia
	Joshua, the high priest, is the religious leader
520	Haggai and Zechariah prophesy (Ezra 5:1; Hag. 1:1)
	Temple construction is resumed (Ezra 5:2; Hag. 1:14-15)
516	The temple is completed (Ezra 6:14-15)
483-458	Esther is queen in Persia
458	Ezra leads a second group of Jews from Babylon to Jerusalem

446	Enemies force the Jews to stop building the walls and virtually destroy the parts already built (Ezra 4:23)
445	Nehemiah leads a third group of exiles back to Jerusalem
	Nehemiah is appointed by Artaxerxes to be governor of Judah
444	Walls are completed
433	Nehemiah goes to Babylon on business (Neh. 2:6; 5:14; 13:6)
432-425	Malachi prophesies during Nehemiah's absence
425	Nehemiah returns from Babylon (Neh. 13:7)

THE GUIDE

CHAPTER ONE

THE BIBLE
AS A WHOLE

THE BIBLE

BIBLE BOOK

THE BIBLE AS A WHOLE

INTRODUCTION

The origin of the Bible

The human side

The Bible is a compilation of sixty-six books, written by forty authors over a period of 1600 years. The authors were from all walks of life: shepherds, farmers, fishermen, tax collectors and kings.

The divine side

When one is discussing the authorship of the Bible, it is never enough to talk only about its human authors. Behind these human authors stands God himself who inspired them to write (2 Tim. 3:16-17; 2 Peter 1:21).

The central theme of the Bible

One of the most fascinating aspects of the Bible is its unity. While many authors contributed to it, all their writings are connected with one theme: the redemption of sinful men and women through the work of the Lord Jesus Christ. A shorter way of stating this theme is 'Paradise lost and regained'.

As the Bible opens, we find God creating Adam and Eve and placing them in a paradise called the garden of Eden. There they were in perfect harmony with God, with each other and with the whole created order. But they did not continue in that state. Because they sinned against God, they not only lost their paradise (Gen. 3:24), but they also brought sin upon the whole human race (Rom. 5:12).

The good news of the Bible is this: God did not leave guilty sinners to themselves. He made a way to redeem a vast multitude from the effects of sin and to restore for them what they lost through sin. That way is his Son, Jesus Christ (John 14:6).

Because of sin, the way to the tree of life was closed in Genesis 3:24. Because of Jesus it is opened again in Revelation 22:2.

In the light of all this, we can shorten the theme even more by merely saying the Bible is a book about the Lord Jesus Christ. The Lord Jesus himself said as much to two of his disciples as he walked with them from Jerusalem to Emmaus on the day of his resurrection. The account tells us that 'He expounded to them in all the Scriptures the things concerning himself' (Luke 24:27; see also vv. 44-45).

We can only study the Bible properly, therefore, by relating all of it to Christ and looking for him in all of it.

To put the theme of the Bible in yet another way, it is the covenant of grace: the covenant in which God pledges salvation to his people on the basis of Christ's atoning death.

The Bible's presentation of its theme

The Bible presents its great theme of salvation through Christ in two 'testaments' or 'covenants': the old and the new. We might say God's covenant of grace is presented in these two subsidiary covenants.

The Old Testament anticipates the coming of the Lord Jesus Christ. The New Testament announces the coming of Christ. It cannot be stressed too strongly that God has always had only one plan of salvation and that is through his Son. The Old Testament is not, therefore, the record of God trying to save people in one way (the law of Moses) and the New Testament the record of him trying another way (Christ). The people of the Old Testament era were saved in exactly the same way as we are, that is, through faith in Christ. The only difference is that they looked forward in faith to what Christ would do, while we look backward in faith to what he has done.

The Old Testament

The Old Testament consists of thirty-nine books. These may be divided into four groups:

Pentateuch
(the word means 'five books' or 'a five-volume book'. These are also called 'The books of Moses' or 'The books of the Law'.)
Genesis
Exodus
Leviticus
Numbers
Deuteronomy

Books of history
(twelve in number and historical in nature)
Joshua, Judges, Ruth, 1 Samuel, 2 Samuel, 1 Kings, 2 Kings, 1 Chronicles, 2 Chronicles, Ezra, Nehemiah, Esther

Books of poetry (five)
Job
Psalms
Proverbs
Ecclesiastes
Song of Solomon

Books of prophecy (seventeen)
Major prophets: Isaiah, Jeremiah, Lamentations, Ezekiel, Daniel (five)

Minor prophets: Hosea, Joel, Amos, Obadiah, Jonah, Micah, Nahum, Habakkuk, Zephaniah, Haggai, Zechariah, Malachi (twelve)

The New Testament

The New Testament consists of twenty-seven books that may be categorized as follows:

Books of history (five)
The Gospels: Matthew, Mark, Luke, John (four)
The Acts of the Apostles (one)

The epistles (twenty-one)
The church epistles of Paul: Romans,
1 Corinthians, 2 Corinthians, Galatians,
Ephesians, Philippians, Colossians,
1 Thessalonians, 2 Thessalonians
and possibly Hebrews (ten)

The pastoral or personal epistles of Paul:
1 Timothy, 2 Timothy, Titus, Philemon (four)

The general epistles: James, 1 Peter, 2 Peter,
1 John, 2 John, 3 John,
Jude (seven)
(written by the men whose names they bear)

The Revelation (one)

Conclusion

What we have seen only constitutes a basic overview of the Bible. In future studies we will take an overview of each of the books of the Bible with a special view to what each one has to offer concerning the Lord Jesus. Our purpose in doing so is not merely to fill our heads with facts about the Bible but to fill our hearts with profound appreciation for the greatness of the salvation God has provided for us.

QUESTIONS FOR DISCUSSION

1. Locate the following verses: 2 Timothy 3:16-17; Hebrews 4:12; 2 Peter 1:16-21. What do they tell us about the Bible?

2. Look at the following verses to see what constitutes a proper response to the Word of God: Psalm 119:161; Isaiah 66:2,5; Acts 17:11; 1 Peter 2:1-3; James 1:22-23. The apostle Paul urged the Colossians to let the word of Christ dwell 'richly' in them — Colossians 3:16. Think about what you can do to obey this command.

3. Do you agree that the central theme of the Bible is the Lord Jesus Christ and his redeeming work? Look up these verses: Luke 24:27,44-47; John 5:45-47; 8:56.

CHAPTER TWO

THE BOOK OF GENESIS

GENESIS

BIBLE BOOK

THE BOOK OF GENESIS

Introduction

INTRODUCTION

Authorship

Genesis is one of the five books attributed to Moses. Mosaic authorship has long been questioned, but 'the whole of Scripture and church history are unified in their adherence to the Mosaic authorship of Genesis'.[1]

Purpose

The book of Genesis is the book of beginnings or origins. The beginning of the world, the human race, the family, sin in the world, death, the nations of the world and the Hebrew race are all presented here. It also contains, of course, the beginning in human history of God's plan of redemption.

Structure

Genesis is easily outlined. It falls into two major parts, each with four subdivisions.

1. Four major events — mankind in general (1:1 - 11:32)
   a. Creation (1:1 - 2:25)
   b. The Fall of Man (3:1-24)
   c. The great flood (6:1 - 9:29)
   d. The tower of Babel (11:1-9)

2. Four great persons — the patriarchs of Israel (12:1 - 50:26)
   a. Abraham (12:1 - 25:34)
   b. Isaac (26:1-34)
   c. Jacob (27:1 - 37:36)
   d. Joseph (39:1 - 50:26)

Overview

Four major events — mankind in general (1:1 - 11:32)

Creation (1:1 - 2:25). The Bible does not yield to our craving for details about God's creative work. It asserts in plain, unadorned language that the universe is not here by accident, but rather by the design of God. Four main truths are emphasized in the creation account:

1. God created out of nothing (1:1)
2. God created by speaking (1:3,9,14,20,24,26,29)
3. God created everything good (1:31)
4. God created man in his image (1:26-28). This is not a reference to the bodies of Adam and Eve because God is a spirit and does not have a body. It means

they were made as spiritual beings capable of fellowship with God, and they were given dominion to rule over creation for God.

The Fall of Man (3:1-24). God gave Adam and Eve a single commandment. They were not to eat of the tree of knowledge of good and evil (2:16-17). This was not some sort of magical tree. God could just as easily have commanded them not to cross a river or enter a cave. The point is that God had given Adam and Eve freedom of will. A free will did not mean anything unless there was a choice to be made. That tree represented a choice. Adam and Eve could refuse to eat of it and thus express their love for God. Or they could eat of it and rebel against God.

Adam and Eve refused to obey, and, in so doing, brought sin upon themselves and upon all their descendants (Rom. 5:12). Because of their sin Adam and Eve died spiritually as soon as they disobeyed God, and they were destined to die physically and eternally. All of us come into this world in the grip of spiritual death and doomed to die physically and eternally.

God could have left Adam and Eve and all their offspring in sin, but he did not. He came to Adam and Eve, who were hiding from him, gave them the first promise of redemption (3:15), and made coverings for them by killing animals (3:21). In killing those animals, God was stating some vital truths:

1. In order to stand in my holy presence, you must be clothed.
2. There is absolutely nothing you can do to clothe yourselves acceptably.
3. I will provide what is necessary for you to stand before me.
4. What I provide to clothe you and make you accept-able to me must involve the shedding of blood. (God had said the penalty for sin is death. If sinners are ever to regain paradise, the penalty for their sin must be paid, either by the sinners themselves or by some-one in their stead. By killing these innocent animals in place of Adam and Eve, God was pointing ahead to the coming of the perfect substitute, his Son, who would die in the place of sinners.)

The great flood (6:1 - 9:29). The account of the flood shows us that sin, from its tiny beginning in the gar-den of Eden, continued to increase and abound until God finally sent the devastating flood. The flood be-comes a lasting emblem of the wrath of God that will finally be expressed against sinners who refuse to em-brace God's plan of salvation. As we study this portion of Genesis, however, we see more than wrath. We see also the patience of God in delaying the judgement so long, the mercy of God in providing a way of escape for Noah and his family, the sovereignty of God in send-ing the flood, and the faithfulness of God to his promises.

The Tower of Babel (11:1-9). This episode is yet another indication of the sinfulness of the human race. After the flood, God commanded Noah's descendants not to stay in one place (9:1); but they built the tower to avoid doing the very thing God wanted, that is, to spread over the whole earth. God frustrated their plans by confusing their language. He is not opposed to unity, but is opposed to a unity that is built around opposition to himself.

Four great people — the patriarchs of Israel (12:1 - 50:26)

Abraham (12:1 - 25:34). God had promised a Redeemer for that human race. The Redeemer had to come from a nation. With Abraham, the Lord began a new nation, the nation of Israel. His promise to bless all the nations of the earth through Abraham was a reaffirmation of the coming Redeemer (12:1-3). That Redeemer was to spring from a son that Abraham would father and his wife Sarah would bear (Gen. 17:15-19). For many years it looked as if that promise could not possibly be fulfilled, but it was, and, in fulfilling it, God taught Abraham, and all believers since, to believe his promises even when they appear to be incapable of fulfilment.

Isaac (26:1-35). Isaac is the least prominent of the Genesis patriarchs. He did, however, receive confirmation of the covenant God made with his father (26:2-5).

TEACHING

Jacob (27:1 - 37:36). Jacob received the name 'Israel' (32:28), which subsequently became the name for the Jewish nation. He was also the father of the twelve sons who became the heads of the twelve tribes of Israel. One of these tribes was, of course, designated as the tribe from which the Messiah would come (49:8-12).

Joseph (39:1 - 50:26). Joseph was used of God to be the means to take the people of Israel into Egypt where they could grow into a great nation. His life was also designed by the Lord to be one of the greatest of all the types of Christ. A type is a person, event or institution of the Old Testament that pictures or prefigures the Lord Jesus Christ. Some of the major similarities between Joseph and Christ are as follows:

1. beloved of their fathers
2. sent to their brethren
3. hated and conspired against by their brethren
4. faithful in hardship and highly exalted after hardship.

QUESTIONS FOR DISCUSSION

1. *Read Psalm 8:1-9; 19:1-6; Isaiah 40:12-31; 45:7,18-19. What attributes of God are put on display in the created order? What is an appropriate response to God's work of creation?*

DISCUSS IT

2. *Read Romans 1:18-32; 3:9-23; 5:12. What do these passages teach us about human nature?*

3. *Read 2 Corinthians 5:21; Hebrews 4:14-16; 1 Peter 2:21-24; 1 John 3:4-5. Was the Lord Jesus Christ free from sin? Is this important in the scheme of redemption? Why?*

CHAPTER THREE

THE BOOK OF EXODUS

EXODUS

THE BOOK OF EXODUS

Introduction

The word 'Exodus' means 'going out' or 'departure'. The book of Exodus recounts how the people of Israel came to be enslaved in Egypt and how the Lord delivered them and established them as a nation.

Although the book itself nowhere claims to be authored by Moses, the Lord Jesus Christ consistently attributed it to him (Mark 7:10; 12:26; Luke 20:37; John 5:46,47; 7:19,22,23).

Purpose

Exodus shows how God fulfilled his promises to Abraham to multiply his descendants into a great nation before bringing them out of Egypt. It also records the beginning of the Passover and the constituting of Israel into a nation.

In setting forth these things, Exodus underscores for us the sovereign grace and power of the Lord God. It was his grace alone that caused

INTRODUCTION

him to choose Israel as his covenant nation, and it was his power that delivered them.

Structure

1. God delivers Israel from bondage in Egypt (1:1 - 15:21)
2. God sustains Israel in the wilderness (15:22 - 18:27)
3. God speaks to Israel at Sinai (19:1 - 40:38)

Overview

God delivers Israel from bondage in Egypt (1:1 - 15:21)

The Lord uses a burning but unconsumed bush to call Moses as Israel's leader. Moses asks for the Lord's name and the Lord responds: 'I AM WHO I AM' (3:13-14). The Lord is the self-existent, self-sufficient, eternal God.

Having been called by the Lord, Moses presents himself to Pharaoh and demands the release of Israel, only to be rebuffed. The Lord then sends nine plagues upon Egypt (7:14 - 10:29). These plagues demonstrate his power to the Egyptians and his sovereignty over their gods. Pharaoh responds to each of these plagues with hardness of heart.

The tenth and decisive plague consisted of the Lord sending his death angel over the land of Egypt at midnight to kill all the firstborn of the land (11:1-6). The people of Israel would be graciously spared from this terrible judgement by putting the blood of un-blemished lambs above and on the sides of their doors (12:7). They were then to stay inside their houses and eat the lambs, along with unleavened bread and bitter herbs (12:8). They would be safe in doing so because the death angel would pass over them when he saw the blood on the doors. In this way the Jewish Passover was instituted.

This devastating judgement persuaded Phar-aoh to let the people of Israel go, but soon he had a change of heart and pursued them. The Lord again intervened on behalf of his people by opening the Red Sea before them and caus-ing them to pass through it on dry land. Phar-aoh and his army attempted to do the same but drowned as the Lord caused the waters to cover them (14:1-31).

*God sustains Israel in the wilderness (15:22 -
18:27)*

After delivering the Israelites from Egypt, the Lord sustained them by providing water (15:22-27; 17:1-7) and manna for them (16:1-36), and by giving them victory over the Amalekites (17:8-16).

God speaks to Israel at Sinai (19:1 - 40:38)

The Lord delivered the people of Israel so that they could be his covenant people. In this section he calls Moses to ascend Mount Sinai to receive the law by which the people were to be governed (19:1 - 24:18). The Lord also gives Moses instructions for the building of the tabernacle (25:1 - 40:38).

The law of God consisted of three parts: ceremonial, civil and moral. The ceremonial law provided guidance for Israel's worship. The civil law provided guidance for how Israel was to function as a nation. The moral law consisted of the Ten Commandments (20:1-17). Because these commandments are an expression of God's unchanging character they are eternally valid. They perfectly summarize the whole of our duty towards God and our fellow men.

Many are confused by the law God gave to Israel. From the time Adam and Eve fell into sin, God had promised eternal salvation through the redeeming death of the Lord Jesus Christ (Gen. 3:15). Did the giving of the law mean that God had changed his mind about the way of salvation? Was he now expecting sinners to earn their salvation through the keeping of this law? The apostle Paul assured the Galatians that the giving of the law was part of God's plan of salvation. He writes: 'Is the law then against the promises of God? Certainly not! For if there had been a law given which could have given life, truly righteousness would have been by the law. But the Scripture has confined all under sin, that the promise by faith in Jesus Christ might be given to those who believe' (Gal. 3:21-22).

The law was given, then, to show us how holy God is, how sinful we are, and, therefore, how desperately we need the righteousness provided by Christ and his redeeming death on behalf of his people.

The sinfulness of human nature is written large in Exodus. While Moses was on the mountain receiving the law of God, the people below were worshipping a golden calf (32:1-35).

Anticipations of Christ

The Passover

Exodus abounds in pictures and types of the Lord Jesus Christ. The Passover is, of course, the major type of Christ (1 Cor. 5:7).

We are by nature under the sentence of eternal death even as the firstborn of Egypt was under the sentence of physical death. But through Christ we have deliverance. He is the Lamb of God (John 1:29) who was without spot, that is, without sin (1 Peter 1:19). All those who take refuge in Christ and rest in faith upon his atoning death are safe. They will not be visited by God's eternal wrath but will be passed over.

The exodus

Israel's departure from Egypt prefigured Christ leading his people out of sin and condemnation into spiritual life. The exodus also prefigured Jesus himself coming out of Egypt after his

TEACHING

parents had taken him there to escape the murderous intentions of Herod (Matt. 2:13-15).

The manna

Christ is the true bread from heaven that gives eternal life to all those who believe in him (John 6:48-58).

The rock

The rock which miraculously produced water for the Israelites (17:1-7) prefigures the Lord Jesus Christ as the Rock that produces the water of eternal life (1 Cor. 10:4).

The tabernacle

The tabernacle was the means by which God dwelt among the people of Israel. This anticipated the Lord Jesus Christ in whom God himself tabernacled among men (John 1:14). The sacrifices offered at the tabernacle pictured the Lord Jesus as the perfect sacrifice for sinners, and the High Priest who carried out the ceremony is a type of Jesus as our high priest (Heb. 4:14 - 5:11).

QUESTIONS FOR DISCUSSION

1. *Have believers in Christ experienced a deliverance from bondage even as the Israelites did under Moses? Read these passages — Matthew 1:21; John 8:34-36; 1 Thessalonians 1:10; 2 Timothy 2:24-26; Hebrews 2:14-15.*

DISCUSS IT

2. *While believers are not saved by keeping the Ten Commandments, are they to practise those commandments with the understanding that they constitute God's unchanging will? Read Romans 13:8-10; 1 Corinthians 7:19; Galatians 5:6; 6:15; Ephesians 4:25 - 6:4; James 2:11-12.*

3. *Does God sustain his people today as he did the people of Israel in the wilderness? Consider the following: 2 Corinthians 1:3-4; 12:9; Hebrews 13:5-6.*

CHAPTER FOUR

THE BOOK OF LEVITICUS

LEVITICUS

THE BOOK OF LEVITICUS

Introduction

INTRODUCTION

Authorship

The book of Leviticus is the third of those known as the 'books of Moses'. The authorship of Moses is explicitly affirmed by the book a total of fifty-six times and is also endorsed by the Lord Jesus Christ (Matt. 8:2-4).

Purpose

Leviticus is a book of laws and regulations by which the people of Israel were to conduct their lives and their worship. The Greek translation of this book had the title '*Leuitikon*', which means 'that which pertains to the Levites'. The Latin version translated this to 'Leviticus', a name that was retained by the English versions, and which reflects the fact that much of the book concerns the ministry of the priests who were of the tribe of Levi.

Uniqueness

No other book of the Bible contains as many words from God himself. Eighty-three statements refer to God speaking.

Structure

1. The offerings (1:1 - 7:38)
2. The priests (8:1 - 10:20; 21:1 - 22:33)
3. The people (11:1 - 15:33; 18:1 - 20:27)
4. The Day of Atonement (16:1 - 17:16)
5. The festivals (23:1 - 26:46)
6. The vows (27:1-34)

Types of Christ

The offerings

The burnt offering (1:3-17; 6:8-13). The burnt offering represented complete dedication to God. A young bull, lamb, goat, turtledove, or young pigeon could be used, but the animal had to be a perfect and complete specimen. The burnt offering depicted his complete dedication to God and his being completely consumed by the fire of God's judgement on the cross.

The meal offering (2:1-16; 6:14-18; 7:12-13). This offering was from the harvest of the land. It had to be finely ground to remove all coarseness. It accompanied all burnt offerings and signified thanksgiving to God. The grain offering typified Christ's humanity in that there was no coarseness or taint of evil in it.

The peace offering (3:1-17; 7:11-21,28-34). A bull, lamb or goat could be used. Part of it was offered to God, part (the breast and thigh) was taken by the priest, and part was eaten by the worshipper. It was, therefore, a shared offering. The peace offering anticipated the peace that comes between God and sinners as a result of Christ's atoning death.

The sin offering (4:1 - 5:13; 6:24-30). The focus of this offering was the purification of the sinner himself. The sin offering prefigures Christ as our sin-bearer (2 Cor. 5:21).

The trespass offering (5:1-19; 7:1-10). This offering addressed sinful acts against the holy things of God (5:15-16), against things 'forbidden' (5:17-19), and against a neighbour's rights and property (6:2-7): sins that required restitution. It typifies Christ making restitution for our sin.

The animals

Even the animals that were used for sacrifices typified Christ:

1. the ox — Christ, the burdened one
2. the sheep — Christ, the silent one
3. the goat — Christ, the sinless one
4. the dove — Christ, the gentle one
5. the pigeon — Christ, the enduring one

The high priest

Sinful men and women cannot approach a holy God without a mediator. The high priest of Leviticus foreshadows the priestly work of the Lord Jesus Christ (Heb. 4:14-15; 7:26-28), the only true mediator between God and man (1 Tim. 2:5).

The Day of Atonement

In the seventh month of the Hebrew calendar (our October) came the most important day of the year for the people of Israel, the day in which atonement was made by the high priest for the sins of the people. This atonement is one of the greatest types of Christ to be found in the Old Testament.

1. As the high priest put off his regular garments, so Christ laid aside his glory and put on our humanity.

2. As the high priest used two goats, one to slay for the people and one to drive away into the wilderness, so Christ died for the sins of his people, and, in doing so, carried their sins so far away they will never be remembered.

3. As the high priest alone performed his duties, so Christ alone made atonement for sinners.

4. As the burning of the skins and flesh of the animals used for sacrifice was taken outside the camp, so Christ went outside the city of Jerusalem to be consumed with the fire of God's wrath (Heb. 13:11-12).

While the Day of Atonement prefigured Christ in many ways, there are distinctions to be drawn:

1. The high priest offered the blood of an involuntary substitute, while Christ voluntarily offered himself.

2. While the high priest had to first make atonement for himself, Christ, who was guilty of no sin, did not (1 Peter 1:19).

3. While the high priest had to make the atonement each year, Christ made it once and for all (Heb. 9:25-28).

4. While the high priest entered an earthly sanctuary, the Lord Jesus entered into heaven itself as our High Priest and did so by virtue of his shed blood (Heb. 9:11-15; 23-24).

5. While the high priest entered the Most Holy Place of the tabernacle as a representative of

his people, Christ has gone into heaven as the forerunner of his people (Heb. 6:19-20), that is, his presence there assures their presence there as well.

Conclusion

It is obvious from what we have seen that Leviticus is
a book about the unrelenting holiness of God, the
exceeding sinfulness of sin and the need for redemption. It is also important to note the following major
themes:

Holiness

We must never forget that the purpose of the Lord's
redeeming death was to free his people from their sins.
His people are called, therefore, to be a holy people.
As Leviticus called for the people of Israel to have clean
foods, bodies, clothes, houses and relationships, so the
Lord calls his people today to be holy (Titus 2:11-14;
1 Peter 1:13-17).

Worship

As the people of Israel had their appointed seasons to
gather and express praise for their redeeming God, so
believers today are commanded to gather and worship
God and to make the atoning death of Christ central in
their worship.

DISCUSS IT

1. *Hebrews 9:22 says ' ...without shedding of blood there is no remission'. Why does God require the shedding of blood to forgive sin? Think of the blood as representing life poured out in death. Think about death as the penalty for sin. Why was it necessary for Jesus to die? Read Isaiah 53:4-12; Romans 3:24-26; 2 Corinthians 5:19-21; Hebrews 2:17; 1 Peter 2:21-24; 3:18; 1 John 4:10.*

2. *Read Romans 12:1-2. What incentive do God's people have to be holy? What can they do to be holy?*

CHAPTER FIVE

THE BOOK OF
NUMBERS

NUMBERS

THE BOOK OF NUMBERS

Introduction

INTRODUCTION

Numbers, the fourth of the 'books of Moses', received its title from the two numberings of the people it reports (1:1 - 4:49; 26:1-65).

The book of Leviticus constitutes an interruption in the narrative of the people of Israel, which Numbers resumes. It relates the census, the organization of the people, the march to Canaan, the spying of Canaan, the unbelief of the people, the judgement of God, the wandering of Israel, the death of the old generation, the census of the new generation.

Numbers is, therefore, the description of the failure of the generation that came out of Egypt. As someone has noted, it is an account of 'the longest funeral march in history'. Only Caleb and Joshua, because of their faithfulness to God, were permitted to finally enter the land of Canaan.

Structure

The book of Numbers lends itself to the following division:

1. The old generation (1:1 - 21:35)
   a. Preparation to advance (1:1 - 10:36)
   b. Failure to advance (11:1 - 21:35)

2. The new generation (22:1 - 36:13)
   a. Their journeying (22:1 - 25:18; 33:1-56)
   b. Their numbering (26:1-65)
   c. Their offerings (28:1 - 30:16)
   d. Their dividing the inheritance (27:1-23; 31:1 - 36:13)

The major episode

The Israelites whom the Lord delivered from bondage in Egypt were well trained in the faithfulness and the power of the Lord. The Lord had promised to deliver them from Egypt and had done so, by showering plague after plague upon the Egyptians and by miraculously opening the Red Sea. The Lord had further demonstrated his faithfulness and power by providing food and water for them in the wilderness (Exod. 16-17).

With this schooling in place, the people of Israel should have had no doubts at all that the Lord would give them the land of Canaan as he had promised (Gen. 12:1-3; 15:7-21; 26:2-3; 28:13-15).

From Israel's camping place in the Wilderness of Paran (12:16), Moses sent twelve men into the land of Canaan to 'spy out' the land (13:17). These spies returned with a majority report and a minority report. The majority (ten spies) reported that the land was everything God had said, but that the people there were far too strong for Israel to conquer. They were particularly troubled by the presence of giants in the land (13:26-29,31-33). Two spies, Joshua and Caleb, acknowledged the presence of these giants, but they had no doubt that their army was well able to defeat them (13:30; 14:6-10). The same God who had delivered them from Egypt would have no difficulty in giving them the land.

Amazingly, the people of Israel turned on Joshua and Caleb and threatened to stone them. At this point, the Lord intervened (14:10) and announced that the people would wander in the wilderness until all of them died except Joshua and Caleb. This wandering was to last forty years, one year for each day the spies spent investigating the land (14:20-35).

The failure of Israel to enter the land is the major episode of Numbers. It serves as a lasting reminder of the importance of believing God's Word and living in obedience to it. Nothing insults God more than our refusal to believe him.

Other themes

1. The evil of rebelling against God and the leaders he appoints (11:1-15; 16:1 - 17:13)
2. The possibility of being closely associated with the things of God without having a heart changed by God (e.g. the mixed multitude — Exod. 12:38; Num. 11:4; and Korah — Num. 16)

3. The danger of God's people being joined with the world (25:1-18).

Foreviews of Christ

As we study the Old Testament, we must never lose sight of the special nature of the people of Israel. Israel was the nation to which God had given the promise of the Messiah. When we study its history, then, we must always keep this in mind. God did not record its history merely because he had some quaint, inexplicable interest in this little nation. His interest in Israel was as a vehicle of his plan of redemption.

The book of Numbers contains two major anticipations of Christ's redemptive work.

The brazen serpent (21:1-9)

The Lord sent poisonous serpents into the camp as a judgement upon the people for their murmuring against him. When the people cried out for deliverance, God instructed Moses to erect a serpent of brass in the midst of the camp. All who looked upon that serpent would be healed of the bite of the poisonous serpents. This remedy typified the Lord Jesus in the following ways:

1. The remedy was not Moses' idea but God's. Salvation from sin is not produced by men but only by God.
2. The remedy consisted of Moses making a serpent in the form of the poisonous serpents. The Lord Jesus

Christ was made in the form of sinful men (Phil. 2:8).

3. As the serpent of brass had no venom, so Christ had no sin (2 Cor. 5:21).

4. As the serpent of brass was lifted up on a pole, so Christ was lifted up on the cross (John 3:14).

5. All that was necessary for the people to be healed of the poisonous bites was to look at the brass serpent, and all that is necessary for healing of sin is to look to Christ.

6. As there was only one remedy for the people of Israel, the serpent on the pole, so there is only one way of eternal salvation, Jesus Christ.

The prophecy of Balaam (22:1 - 24:25)

Balak, king of Moab, was extremely frightened by Israel (22:3-4) and hired the prophet Balaam to pronounce a curse on her (22:5-7). Each time Balaam sought to curse the nation of Israel, however, he ended up pronouncing a blessing. In the midst of his fourth oracle, he spoke of seeing a 'Star' coming out of Judah and a 'Sceptre' out of Israel (24:17). The Lord Jesus Christ is 'the Bright and Morning Star' (Rev. 22:16) whose birth was accompanied by a star (Matt. 2:2). He is also the king who holds the sceptre of righteousness (Heb. 1:8).

The budding of Aaron's rod (17:1-13), the rock (20:1-13, cf. 1 Cor. 10:4), and the cities of refuge (35:9-34) are also considered types of Christ.

QUESTIONS FOR DISCUSSION

1. *What attributes of God are prominently displayed in the book of Numbers? Read the following: Numbers 12:9-16; 14:11-35; 16:20-45; 21:4-9.*

2. *Read Hebrews 3:1 - 4:16. What warnings and exhortations does the author give his readers from Israel's experiences in the wilderness?*

THE GUIDE

CHAPTER SIX

THE BOOK OF DEUTERONOMY

DEUTER-
ONOMY

BIBLE BOOK

THE BOOK OF DEUTERONOMY

Introduction

Moses is very prominent in this book. His name appears thirty-six times, and he speaks in the first person four times (1:16,18; 3:21; 29:5).

While Mosaic authorship has been attacked by higher critics, the Lord Jesus Christ did not hesitate to affirm it (Matt. 19:7-9; John 5:45-47).

It is noteworthy that the book of Deuteronomy is quoted ninety times in fourteen New Testament books. The most striking of these is our Lord's quotations when he was tempted by Satan (Matt. 4:4,7,10).

Purpose

The word 'Deuteronomy' means 'second law'. In this book, Moses reminds the people of Israel of the law God gave them on Mount Sinai.

It is not hard to understand why this was necessary. There had been a change of generations since the first giving of the law. The generation that came out of Egypt had refused to enter the land of Canaan, and God caused them to wander in the wilderness for a period of forty years. All were now dead except for Moses, Joshua and Caleb. Because Moses himself was now about to die, it was essential that the new generation be reminded that their future would be determined by their obedience to the law of God.

Structure

Introduction (1:1-5)
1. Sermons (1:5 - 31:29)
    a. Moses' first sermon (1:5 - 4:43)
    b. Moses' second sermon (4:44 - 28:68)
    c. Moses' third sermon (29:1 - 31:29)
2. Appendices (31:30 - 34:12)
    a. Moses' song (31:30 - 32:43)
    b. Moses' final blessing (32:44 - 33:29)
    c. Moses' death (34:1-12)

Overview

Introduction (1:1-5)

As Deuteronomy opens, the children of Israel are camped once again on the border of the land of Canaan. They had been there before but had failed to enter the land because of their unbelief and had been destined

by the Lord to wander in the wilderness for forty years (Num. 14:32-34).

Sermons (1:5 - 30:20)

Moses' first sermon (1:5 - 4:43). In this sermon, Moses reviews some of the major events in Israel's history (1:5 - 3:29). He also issues a clarion call to obedience (4:1-14) and warns against idolatry (4:15-40).

Moses' second sermon (4:44 - 28:68). The longest of Moses' three sermons is a sustained exposition and application of the laws of God. It begins with a review of the Ten Commandments (5:1-22).

This section also includes the '*Shema*', which is the Hebrew word for 'hear' (6:4-9). The Shema reminded the people that their God was the only true God, that they were to love him with all their hearts, souls and strength, and that they were to hold God's commandments in their hearts and diligently teach them to their children.

Moses also points the people to the basis of their covenant relationship with God. It was not because they were worthy and deserving but rather because of God's grace (7:6-8). It has always been so. Those who know God can take credit for nothing. God chose them before the foundation of the world, called them unto himself and gave them the faith with which they believe (Rom. 8:29-30; Eph. 1:3-6; Phil. 1:29).

Moses concluded his second sermon by revealing to the people a ceremony that they were to observe when they finally possessed Canaan (27:11). They were to gather from time to time on two mountains with a small valley between, a setting that provided a natural amphitheatre. Six of their tribes were to stand on Mount Ebal and the other six tribes on Mount Gerizim. Some of the Levites were to stand in the valley between the two mountains and call out the cursings and the blessings. When they said something was cursed, the tribes on Mount Ebal would respond with an 'Amen'. When they said something was blessed, the tribes on Mount Gerizim would respond with an 'Amen'.

Moses included in these instructions a list of the blessings the people could expect to enjoy through obedience (28:1-14) and a long list of the curses they could expect to experience through disobedience (28:15-68). Obedience is not something that God expected from Israel alone, but from every generation of God's people. Obeying God is not always easy, but its yoke is light compared to that of sin and judgement.

Moses' third sermon (29:1 - 31:29). Moses here renews God's covenant with the people (29:1 - 30:20) and announces his impending death and Joshua as his successor (31:1-29).

Appendices (31:30 - 34:12)

Moses' song (31:30 - 32:43). Moses praises the Lord for being the Rock upon whom his people can rest (vv. 4,15,18,30-31). He is also as tender towards his people as an eagle hovering over its young (v. 11) and far more capable of protecting them.

With such a God it would seem that the people Israel would never be inclined to stray from him, but Moses knew they would and, therefore, included stern warnings against idolatry and the Lord's determination to judge it (vv. 15-42).

Moses' final blessing (32:44 - 33:29). After pronouncing blessings on the individual tribes of the nation, Moses rejoices in the sovereign majesty of God (33:26-29). He concludes with this exclamation:

> Happy are you, O Israel!
> Who is like you,
> a people saved by the LORD...
>
> (33:29).

How little we, as the children of God, realize how blessed we are to be 'saved by the Lord'!

Moses' death (34:1-12). After viewing the land that the Lord would give to Israel, Moses died and was buried in an unknown place by the Lord himself. Warren Wiersbe observes: 'When your time comes to die, the important thing is not the grandeur of your funeral but the greatness of your life.'[1]

An anticipation of Christ

The Lord Jesus Christ is the prophet of whom Moses spoke in Deuteronomy 18:15-19. In fact, Jesus would hold a threefold office: as prophet he would perfectly declare the Word of God; as priest he would offer himself as the sacrifice for the sins of his people; as king he would reign from heaven until all his enemies are subdued.

There has never been a prophet like Jesus. He, the eternal Son of God, would come 'from among their brethren' (18:18) by taking unto himself our humanity. He would speak the words which the Father put in his mouth (18:18), words of life, truth and grace. Salvation comes only to those who hear and heed his words. Those who refuse to do so will face the unbearable wrath of God (18:19).

QUESTIONS FOR DISCUSSION

1. *Read the following — Matthew 7:28-29; Luke 4:22; John 7:45-46. What do these verses tell us about the prophetic ministry of the Lord Jesus Christ? Read Jesus'*

'Bread of Life' discourse in John 6:26-58. What truths did Jesus proclaim in this portion of his prophetic ministry?

2. Read Hebrews 11:23-29. What made Moses the great man of God that he was?

3. Moses' preaching in the book of Deuteronomy reminded a new generation of what God had done for their fathers. Is it vital for Christian leaders to remind God's people of what God has done for them? Consider 2 Peter 1:12-15; 3:1-4.

THE GUIDE

CHAPTER SEVEN

THE BOOK OF JOSHUA

JOSHUA

THE BOOK OF JOSHUA

Introduction

INTRODUCTION

The book of Joshua brings us to the second major division of the Old Testament, that is, the historical books. This section, consisting of twelve books, takes us from the nation of Israel entering the land of Canaan under Joshua to the division of the nation into two kingdoms and their subsequent captivity.

Joshua, the author of most of this book and after whom it was named, was Moses' successor as the leader of Israel. He and Caleb were, as God had promised, the only Israelites who survived the forty years of wandering in the wilderness. That period ended with the selection of Joshua to lead Israel and with the death of Moses (Deut. 34).

Joshua is the book of conquest. It opens with Israel poised to do what she should have done forty years earlier, namely, begin the invasion of Canaan. It closes with Israel in possession of most of the land and with only a few enemies remaining.

Structure

The book of Joshua may be outlined as follows:

1. Entering the land (1:1 - 5:15)
   a. The Lord prepares (Joshua 1:1-9)
   b. Joshua prepares Israel (1:10 - 5:15)
      i. militarily (1:10 - 5:1)
      ii. spiritually (5:2-15)
2. Taking the land (6:1 - 12:24)
   a. The central campaign (6:1-8)_
   b. The southern campaign (9:1 - 10:43)
   c. The northern campaign (11:1-15)
   d. Summary (11:16 - 12:24)
3. Dividing the land (13:1 - 22:34)
   a. Special allotments (13:1 - 14:15)
   b. Major allotments (15:1 – 19:51)
   c. Special provisions (20:1 - 22:34)
4. Keeping the land (23:1 - 24:33)
   a. Joshua's first speech (23:1-16)
   b. Joshua's second speech (24:1-28)
5. Conclusion (24:29-33)

Major themes

The faithfulness of God to his promises

God's promise to give his people the land. Centuries before Joshua came along, God had promised Abraham that he would give the land of Canaan to his descendants (Gen. 12:7; 15:18-21). That promise looked very uncertain after Israel refused to enter the land under Moses. But forty years later the promise was fulfilled even to the point that Joshua was able to say: 'Not a word failed of any good thing which the LORD had spoken to the house of Israel. All came to pass' (21:45, see also 23:14). God's promises can never finally be defeated or thwarted by human wickedness.

God's promise to judge the Canaanite nations for their wickedness. The Canaanite nations whom Israel defeated and deposed were extremely wicked and had provoked God for centuries (Gen. 15:16; Lev. 18:24-30; Deut. 9:4-5; 18:9-14).

The sovereign power and majesty of God

The crossing of Jordan (3:1-17). The Lord miraculously opened the Jordan River while it was at floodtide, and the people of Israel crossed over on dry land even as their fathers had done when the Lord opened the Red Sea.

The collapse of Jericho (6:1-20). Jericho was considered to be invincible, but the walls of the city fell flat after the people of Israel marched around them once a day for seven days and seven times on the seventh day.

TEACHING

The sun standing still (10:12-14). This miracle seems to have consisted of a retardation of the rotation of the earth so that it required forty-eight hours.

The importance of obedience to God's Word

In addition to demonstrating the sovereignty of God, the crossing of Jordan and the collapse of Jericho show the importance of obeying God. In each situation, the people of Israel were given detailed instructions that they were to follow to the letter. In each case their obedience was rewarded with God's blessing. The importance of obedience is also stressed in the commission of Joshua (1:7-8) and in his addresses (23:11-16; 24:14-25). The terrible consequences of failing to obey God's Word is painfully and powerfully set forth in the account of Achan's sin (7:1-26).

The grace of God

Joshua is also a book about the grace of God. That grace shines and sparkles throughout. The fact that Israel was able to take the land was due to the grace of God. It was not due to Israel's might in taking, but rather due to God giving them the land (23:9-10).

The grace of God is also evident in the story of Rahab, the harlot of Jericho. This account shows us that there was mercy for those among the Canaanite nations who believed his Word (2:1-21).

Spiritual lessons and applications

Through Joshua the people of Israel were, as we have noted, forcefully reminded of the Lord's faithfulness to his promises. The Lord's faithfulness in giving them the land of Canaan had to encourage them to believe that the Lord would be faithful in fulfilling yet another promise, that is, the coming of the Messiah.

The people under Joshua probably did not realize that their leader was himself a type of Christ, but succeeding generations have noted the following parallels:

1. The name 'Joshua' is the Hebrew equivalent of the Greek name 'Jesus' ('Jehovah is salvation').
2. As Joshua succeeded Moses and won the victory unreached by Moses, so Christ succeeded the Mosaic law and won the victory that could not be reached by the law (John 1:17; Rom. 8:2-4; Gal. 3:23-25; Heb. 7:18-19).
3. As Joshua was the captain or commander of Israel, so Jesus is the 'captain' of salvation who will lead 'many sons to glory' (Heb. 2:10). As their captain, he always leads his people in triumph (2 Cor. 2:14; see also Rom. 8:37).
4. As Joshua defeated Israel's enemies and gave her rest in the land, so Jesus has defeated Satan and his forces, and has given his people spiritual rest in this world and eternal rest in the world to come (Heb. 4:1-10).

TEACHING

We must always remember that throughout the Old Testament, God was putting things in place for the coming of his Son. His Son had to come from a nation, and God put that in place by choosing Abraham to be the father of the nation of Israel. With Joshua the Lord gave his people the land where Christ was to be born, where he was to minister and where he was to die on the cross and rise again.

QUESTIONS FOR DISCUSSION

1. The book of Joshua emphasizes God's faithfulness to his promises (21:45; 23:14). What promises do you cherish and especially look forward to seeing fulfilled? Read John 14:1-2; 1 Thessalonians 4:13-18; Revelation 21:2-4; 22:3-5.

2. God expelled the Canaanite nations from the land because of their wickedness. Note the sins of these nations as detailed in Leviticus 18:24-30; Deuteronomy 9:4-5; 18:9-14. Are the sins of those nations prevalent today? If so, what does this tell us about the possibility of God's judgement?

3. The Christian life is one of spiritual warfare. Read Ephesians 6:10-20. Who are the enemies of the Christian? What constitutes the armour of the Christian?

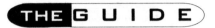

THE GUIDE

CHAPTER EIGHT

THE BOOKS OF JUDGES AND RUTH

JUDGES & RUTH

THE BOOKS OF JUDGES AND RUTH

JUDGES

Introduction

INTRODUCTION

The book takes its name from the individuals God raised up to lead the nation of Israel and to deliver her from her enemies. No author is named, but it is traditionally attributed to Samuel. It was quite obviously written after the nation of Israel had appointed a king. The recurring phrase 'in those days there was no king in Israel' clearly implies that the author wrote when there was a king. In all likelihood, then, Samuel wrote this book after he retired from his own tenure as judge and while Saul, Israel's first king, was reigning.

The central theme of the book is the failure of the people of God to stay true to him and the subsequent cost of their failures. As such, it constitutes a sad contrast to the book of Joshua, where an obedient people were able to conquer their enemies. In Judges a disobedient people floundered and failed.

Structure

1. A general collapse (1:1 - 3:4)
2. A recurring cycle (3:5 - 16:31)
3. Specific compromises (17:1 - 21:25)
   a. Idolatry (17:1 - 18:31)
   b. Immorality (19:1 - 21:25)

The cycle

A quick glance at the above outline reveals that most of the book is devoted to a recurring cycle. This cycle may be diagrammed in this way:

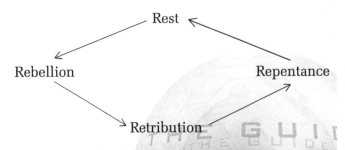

This cycle indicates that the people of Israel, after enjoying peace and tranquillity for a time, would become careless and slip into rebellion against God. God would then judge them by causing one of their enemies to oppress them. The people would then cry out to God in repentance and he would then raise up a judge to deliver them from the enemy and restore them to rest.

We must not miss this point: it was Israel's rebellion against God that brought his hand of judgement upon them. The people had clear commands from God on how they were to live, but this was a time when the commands of God were casually laid aside and 'everyone did what was right in his own eyes' (17:6; 21:25).

The six episodes of this cycle are as follows:

Cycle	Passage	Oppressors	Judge(s)
1	3:8-11	Mesopotamians	Othniel
2	3:12-31	Moabites	Ehud, Shamgar
3	4:1-5:31	Canaanites	Deborah
4	6:1-10:5	Midianites	Gideon, Tola, Jair
5	10:6-12:15	Ammonites	Jephthah, Ibzan,Elon, Abdon
6	13:1-16:31	Philistines	Samson

Major teachings

The book of Judges shows how deeply sin is embedded in human nature and how desperately men need a Saviour. It also shows that human wickedness, no matter how strong, cannot defeat the plan of God. During the era of the judges, Israel strayed far from their covenant with the Lord, but, while he provided correction and chastisement, he did not completely cast them off. Instead he continued to work in them to achieve his announced purpose, namely, to bring the Messiah who would provide the greatest deliverance of all, that is, deliverance from sin. In fact it may be said that all the deliverers of Israel in the book of Judges are types of Christ, the great Redeemer and deliverer of his people.

Anticipations of Christ

The Open Bible observes: 'Each judge is a savior and a ruler, a spiritual and political deliverer. Thus, the judges portray the role of Christ as the Savior-King of his people. The book of Judges also illustrates the need for a righteous king.

'Including First Samuel, seventeen judges are mentioned altogether. Some are warrior-rulers (e.g., Othniel and Gideon), one is a priest (Eli), and one is a prophet (Samuel). This gives a cumulative picture of the three offices of Christ, who excelled all His predecessors in that He was the ultimate Prophet, Priest, and King.'[1]

RUTH

Background

The book of Ruth, one of only two in the Bible that bear the name of women, is set in the period of the judges (1:1). Authorship is often attributed to Samuel, but this is by no means certain.

TEACHING

The story

The story begins with an Israelite family, consisting of Elimelech, Naomi and their two sons, leaving famine-ravaged Israel to stay in Moab. There the two sons find wives, Orpah and Ruth, and there they die along with their father Elimelech. Left with only two daughters-in-law and hearing that the famine at her home in Bethlehem was over, Naomi decided to return. She sought to persuade her daughters-in-law to stay in Moab, but Ruth refused to do so, uttering some of the best-known words in the Bible (1:16-17).

Back in Bethlehem, Ruth met Boaz, whom she discovered to be Naomi's relative ('kinsman') and who, according to the law of Moses, had the right to redeem Naomi's estate, which included the right to marry Ruth. As it turned out, there was a closer relative than Boaz, but he waived his right to redeem Naomi's estate leaving Boaz free to do so. The story ends with Boaz and Ruth being married and with Ruth bearing Obed, the grandfather of David.

Structure

1. Ruth forsakes Moab (1:1-22)
2. Ruth catches Boaz' attention (2:1-23)
3. Ruth requests redemption (3:1-18)
4. Ruth receives redemption (4:1-22)

Major themes

The following are some of the major themes that emerge from the book of Ruth.

1. *The scope of God's redemptive plan.* Ruth the Moabitess illustrates that God's redemptive plan extended beyond the Jews to Gentiles and that women are co-heirs with men of God's grace. Ruth, along with Tamar (Gen. 38), Rahab (Josh. 2) and Bathsheba (2 Sam. 11-12), becomes part of the messianic line.
2. *The beauty of whole-hearted devotion.* Ruth's devotion to Naomi (1:15-18) beautifully pictures the type of devotion Christians should demonstrate in their relationship to the Lord and in their homes.
3. *God's ability to bring good out of evil.* It was not good that Elimelech and his family left the land of Israel. Israelites were commanded to stay in the land even in famines and trust the Lord to sustain them. But even though Elimelech and his family disobeyed, the Lord brought good out of it, namely, Ruth.

A picture of Christ

The kinsman-redeemer of the Old Testament had to meet certain qualifications:

1. He had to be a blood relative.
2. He had to have the money to redeem the inheritance.
3. He had to be willing to redeem the inheritance.

DISCUSS IT

4. He had to be willing to marry the wife of a deceased kinsman.

Christ is our kinsman-Redeemer.

1. He became one of us, sharing our nature.
2. He was able to pay the price demanded of us — perfect obedience to the law of God.
3. He was willing to pay the price to redeem his people, namely, God's judgement.
4. He was willing to make us his bride (Eph. 5:23).

QUESTIONS FOR DISCUSSION

1. Look again at the cycle in Judges. In periods of revival God moves his people directly from the rebellion phase to the repentance phase. Read Hosea 14:1-4. What must we do to return to the Lord?

2. Do God's people today still struggle with obedience to God? Where does disobedience lead? Read Hebrews 12:3-11.

3. Elimelech and Naomi made a bad choice, while Ruth made a good choice. How can we make the right choices in life? Read Psalm 1:1-3; 119:1-3,105; Proverbs 3:5-6.

CHAPTER NINE

THE FIRST BOOK OF SAMUEL

1 SAMUEL

BIBLE BOOK

THE FIRST BOOK OF SAMUEL

Introduction

INTRODUCTION

1 Samuel signals the beginning of three 'double' books of the Old Testament: 1 and 2 Samuel, 1 and 2 Kings, 1 and 2 Chronicles. In the Hebrew manuscripts each of these 'doubles' was one book. These books may be said to present the rise and fall of the Israelite monarchy.

1 Samuel covers a period of about 115 years. It takes us from the birth of the last judge of Israel (Samuel) to the death of the first king (Saul).

Much of the book may very well have been written by Samuel himself with additions being made by one of two prophets: Nathan or Gad (1 Chron. 29:29).

Structure

1 Samuel is the book of three men:

1. Samuel — the last of the judges (1:1 - 10:27)
   a. his consecration (1:1 - 2:26)
   b. his call (3:1-21)

Overview

Samuel

1 Samuel opens with the account of his unusual birth. His mother Hannah prayed fervently for a son and promised to dedicate that son to the Lord. When Samuel was weaned, Hannah kept that pledge by taking him to the priest, Eli, at the tabernacle of the Lord in Shiloh. There Samuel received God's call to be his faithful servant. Samuel obeyed that call by first prophesying against the wicked sons of Eli (ch. 3) and by leading Israel in the ways of the Lord.

Towards the end of Samuel's tenure, the people of Israel demanded that he anoint a king to lead them so they could be like the nations around them (ch. 8). The Lord told Samuel to comply even though it was not his will for Israel to have a king at this time.

Saul

Saul became God's judgement on Israel for demanding a king. His reign started auspiciously enough with a military victory (ch. 11), but Saul soon showed his true colours by flagrantly disobeying the clear commandments of God on two occasions (13:1-14; 15:1-28). Because of Saul's sins, the Lord announced through Samuel that the kingdom would be taken from his family and given to another (15:28). Saul's later life only gave additional evidence of his unfitness to be king as he sought to kill David and went to the witch of Endor for guidance (28:3-25).

David

After announcing that Saul's family would be set aside, the Lord sent Samuel to anoint one of the sons of Jesse to be Saul's successor. After passing over Jesse's other sons, Samuel anointed David (16:1-13). David burst on the public stage by defeating the Philistine giant, Goliath, in battle and delivering Israel from Philistine bondage (17:1-58). Almost immediately Saul became jealous of the attention David received for this victory (18:1-9) and soon began planning to kill him. The Lord, however, protected David and brought him to the throne after Saul was killed in battle (1 Sam. 31 - 2 Sam. 5:5).

Major themes

The terrible results of sin

The sins of Eli and his sons led to their deaths and the loss of the ark to the Philistines (4:1-22). The sin of Israel in asking for a king led to Saul who brought nothing but heartache and disaster (8:4-5,19-20). The sins of Saul led to the kingdom being taken from his family (15:28). In contrast, Samuel's life of faithful obedience to God brought blessing to the whole nation.

The importance of prayer

Hannah and Samuel both shine as examples of prayer (1:10,21,27; 7:5,9; 8:6; 12:23).

The sovereignty of God

Throughout 1 Samuel the sovereign control of God is evident. God sets Saul aside and brings David in as king, and there was nothing Saul or anyone else could do to prevent God from achieving his purpose.

Anticipations of Christ

In his powerful work, *The History of Redemption*, Jonathan Edwards refers to three types of Christ in the Old Testament: institutional, providential and personal.

The animal sacrifices were the greatest of the institutional types; Israel's deliverance from Egypt was the greatest of the providential types; and David was the greatest of the personal types.

The following are some of the major parallels between David and Christ:

1. Both were shepherds from Bethlehem. David shepherded sheep as a young man and the nation as a man. The Lord Jesus Christ is 'the Good Shepherd' who laid down his life for his sheep (John 10:11).

2. As David was anointed by the Lord to rule over Israel, so Christ is the Lord's anointed to rule over his church.

3. As David defeated the giant Goliath with the unlikely instrument of a sling and delivered his people, so the Lord Jesus defeated Satan with the unlikely instrument of a Roman cross and thus delivered his people from their sins.

4. As David was hated and persecuted by Saul so Christ was hated and persecuted in his earthly ministry.

5. As Saul's schemes could not thwart David from coming to the throne of Israel so the

schemes of Satan and wicked men will not be able to thwart God from causing every knee to bow before Christ and every tongue to confess that he is Lord.

QUESTIONS FOR DISCUSSION

1. God sovereignly chose or elected David as king of Israel. Are believers in Christ sovereignly chosen by God unto salvation? Read Romans 8:29-30; Ephesians 1:3-6; 1 Peter 1:1-2.

2. God answered the prayer of Hannah for a son. Read James 5:16-18. What kind of prayer is pleasing to God?

CHAPTER TEN

THE SECOND BOOK OF SAMUEL

THE SECOND BOOK OF SAMUEL

Introduction

While the first book of Samuel is the book about three men, the second book of Samuel is very much the book about one man, David. Israel never had a greater king. His importance is easy to see in the Bible. His name is mentioned 1127 times, 58 of which are in the New Testament. 61 chapters are devoted to a description of his life and reign (1 Sam. 16 - 1 Kings 2; 1 Chron. 11-29).

In addition to those Scriptures that talk about him, several were written by him. 73 of the 150 psalms are directly attributed to him, and it is possible that he wrote some of those which name no author.

Authorship

Authorship of 2 Samuel is usually attributed to one of two prophets, Nathan and Gad, or to a collaboration of the two.

Structure

1. David's triumphs (1:1 - 10:19)
2. David's transgressions (11:1 - 12:15)
3. David's troubles (12:16 - 24:25)

Overview

David's triumphs (1:1 - 10:19)

The second book of Samuel opens with David learning of the death of Saul and his son, Jonathan, in battle against the Philistines.

It would seem that with Saul's death the way was cleared for David to come to the throne of all Israel. But this was not the case. David was immediately selected as king by the tribe of Judah (2:4), but the other tribes of Israel selected one of Saul's sons, Ishbosheth (2:8). This began a period of civil unrest and occasional war in the nation. After a period of seven years, Ishbosheth was assassinated (4:1-12), and David was made king over the entire nation (5:1-3).

With David at the helm, the nation immediately launched into its golden age of success and prosperity. Chief among David's accomplishments were:

1. the conquest of the city of Jerusalem (5:1-10)
2. various building projects (5:9-11)
3. impressive military victories (5:17-25; 8:1-14; 10:1-19)

4. the placing of the ark of the covenant in Jerusalem (6:1-19)

David's transgressions (11:1 - 12:15)

So greatly blessed of God was David that we would expect to read that he lived out his days in faithfulness and devotion to the Lord and continued to experience triumph after triumph. But even the greatest men of God can sin grievously. David did so by engaging in an affair with Bathsheba and by having her husband Uriah killed. David's repentance for these sins and the joy he found in God's forgiveness are set forth in two well-known psalms (32 and 51).

David's troubles (12:16 - 24:25)

For these dreadful sins, David paid a fearful price, just as Nathan the prophet had predicted (12:10). The baby conceived in his affair with Bathsheba died (12:15-19). Another son, Amnon, was murdered by his brother Absalom (13:23-29). Absalom himself led a rebellion against his father and was killed in the process (15:1 - 18:15).

Although David found forgiveness with the Lord, he never did seem to get his 'touch' back for ruling over the kingdom. The book closes with David committing yet another serious sin by numbering the people (24:1-25).

Major themes

The faithfulness of God to his promises

While he was still a young man, David was anointed by Samuel as the future king of Israel (1 Sam. 16). It often looked as if he would never come to the throne. It seemed all but certain that he would not survive when he confronted Goliath and that he would perish during those years that he fled from Saul. When he finally did come to the throne, it was only as king of Judah rather than as king of the whole nation. But through it all God preserved him, and David eventually reigned as king over the entire nation, just as God had promised.

The need to be ever vigilant against sin

Having walked with God for many years, David was still not immune from sin.

The terrible consequences of sin

While God forgave David for his sins, he did not remove the consequences of them. In doing so, God honours his law of sowing and reaping (Gal. 6:7), and teaches us to be more careful about yielding to temptation.

The greatness of God's grace

Although God did not take away the consequences of David's sin, he did truly forgive him (Ps. 32) and continued to use him. God would have been justified in simply setting David aside and bringing another to rule in his place, but God allowed him to continue ruling.

Anticipations of Christ

The high point of David's reign is found in chapter seven. David desired to build a house for the worship of the Lord, but the Lord told David not to do so. David was a man of war who was appointed to secure peace for his nation. With that peace in place, his son would build the temple (7:1-13).

The Lord also used this occasion to announce to David that his throne would be established for ever (7:16). The repeated use of 'for ever' removes the fulfilment of God's promise from any earthly king and attaches it to the one and only eternal king, Jesus Christ. The promise was, therefore, that from David's line, the Messiah himself, the eternal king, would spring. Christ is repeatedly called 'the seed of David' (Rom. 1:3-4; 2 Tim. 2:8) and 'the son of David' (Matt. 9:27; 15:22; 20:30; Mark 10:47; Luke 18:38). Christ, David's great son, is even now reigning in the hearts of his people, and his reign will eventually be acknowledged universally (Phil. 2:9-11).

In addition to receiving this glorious promise from God, David was himself something of a picture or type of Christ. As the triumphant king of the early chapters of 2 Samuel, he pictured the victorious reign of the Lord Jesus Christ. As a man of war, he pictured the Lord Jesus during his earthly ministry in which he was often engaged in conflict with his enemies and eventually secured the peace of his people by defeating Satan and his forces.

David in his transgressions did not, of course, picture Christ. He did at that time, however, show Israel's need of a king who would be perfectly righteous but would also lead his people into righteousness.

QUESTIONS FOR DISCUSSION

1. *David's sins of adultery, deception and murder remind us that even the greatest saints must ever be vigilant against sin. Name some other saints who fell into grievous sin? Read Genesis 9:20-21; 12:10-20; Numbers 20:2-13; John 18:15-27.*

2. *Read David's prayer for forgiveness in Psalm 51. On what basis does he plead for forgiveness? What names does he use for his sin? Against whom was his sin directed? What does he say about his nature?*

3. *Read David's rejoicing in forgiveness in Psalm 32. How often did his sin trouble him? How did he find relief from the guilt of his sin?*

CHAPTER ELEVEN

THE FIRST
BOOK OF KINGS

BIBLE BOOK

THE FIRST BOOK OF KINGS

Introduction

1 and 2 Kings were originally one book. That book was divided into two parts to make its contents more easily accessible.

Each of these two books carries a tremendous message. Together they trace the nation of Israel from her time of greatest glory to her division into two kingdoms and to the captivity of each of those divisions.

1 Kings tells us the first part of this sad story. It may be called the book of disobedience and division. The key verse of this book reads as follows: 'Therefore the LORD said to Solomon, "Because you have done this, and have not kept my covenant and my statutes, which I have commanded you, I will surely tear the kingdom away from you and give it to your servant"' (11:11).

Authorship and purpose

1 Kings has traditionally been considered to be the work of the prophet Jeremiah who lived

during the years preceding the collapse and captivity of the kingdom of Judah. It was probably written during the time when the people of Judah were in captivity for the following purposes:

1. to explain to them why they were there;
2. to remind them that God's faithfulness to his promises ensured their release;
3. to show them how they must live when they finally returned to the land.

Structure

1. The forty-year reign of Solomon over the united kingdom (1:1 - 11:43)
2. The first eighty years of the divided kingdom (12:1 - 22:53)

Overview

The forty-year reign of Solomon over the united kingdom (1:1 - 11:43)

1 Kings opens with David, Solomon's father, still on the throne of Israel and in very feeble condition. Solomon's brother Adonijah sought to take advantage of his father's weakened condition and take the throne for himself, even though David had made it clear that Solomon was to be his successor. These troubles in

David's family remind us that the prophecy of
Nathan regarding David's family continued to
be fulfilled right up to David's death (2 Sam.
12:10).

Adonijah's scheme failed, and Solomon came
to the throne with his father's solemn charge to
obey God (2:1-4).

At first Solomon obeyed this charge and the
blessing of God was poured upon him. God
granted his request for wisdom and also graciously gave him tremendous prosperity and
success (3:5-14). With God's blessing upon him,
Solomon led the nation to unprecedented glory.
The crowning achievement during these years
was the building of the temple (5:1 - 8:66). At
the dedication of the temple, Solomon reminded
the people how important it was for them to continue living in obedience to God (8:57-61). But it
was not long before Solomon's own heart turned
from the Lord to the idols that his foreign wives
worshipped (11:4). Solomon's life serves as a lasting reminder that we never advance so far spiritually that we no longer have to be on our guard
against sin.

It was Solomon's turning from the Lord that
caused the nation to be divided into two kingdoms: the kingdom of Israel consisting of ten
tribes and the kingdom of Judah consisting of
two tribes. The latter kingdom had Jerusalem as
its capital and continued to be ruled by the descendants of David.

The first eighty years of the divided kingdom (12:1 - 22:53)

Perhaps the key word to remember while studying the last half of 1 Kings is 'alternating'. This portion of the book alternates from one kingdom to another to describe events and kings. One must always pay careful attention to which kingdom is being discussed.

The kingdom of Israel

Jeroboam, the head of Solomon's slave labour force, began to reign in Israel after the kingdom divided. Although he had seen the terrible results of Solomon's idolatry, he proceeded to institute a whole new religion around two golden calves (12:25-33). Because of this idolatry, the kingdom of Israel was characterized by trouble and unrest. 1 Kings gives brief summaries of the following kings who ruled after Jeroboam: Nadab (15:25-31), Baasha (15:27 - 16:7), Elah (16:8-10), Zimri (16:9-20), Omri (16:21-28) and Ahab (16:29 - 22:40).

All of these kings were bad, but Ahab was the worst. He and his evil wife Jezebel led the nation of Israel to embrace Baal to an unprecedented degree. It was during the reign of Ahab that God raised up the great prophet Elijah (17:1 - 19:21; 21:1-29).

The kingdom of Judah

The last half of 1 Kings summarizes the reigns of the following kings: Rehoboam (14:21-31), Abijam (15:1-8),

Asa (15:9-24) and Jehoshaphat (22:41-50). The first two were evil, while the last two were good.

It should be noted that 1 Kings only tells part of the story of these two kingdoms and the kings who reigned over them. 2 Kings completes the story.

Major themes

The importance of obedience to God

Time after time it was made clear that the pathway to blessing lay in obedience, that idolatry would bring nothing but heartache; and time after time the kings and the people of the kingdoms, both when united and when divided, chose idolatry.

The faithfulness of God to his promises

1 Kings shows God honouring his promise to keep the line of David alive. God also kept his promises to judge those who turned from him.

The grace and kindness of God

In the midst of wickedness, the Lord demonstrated his grace. The fact that he allowed the two kingdoms to worship idols for so many years was due to his grace. The fact that during this time the Lord raised up many prophets to warn both the kings and the people and call them to repentance was due to his grace.

Anticipations of Christ

1. The glory of Solomon's early reign serves as a faint picture of the glories of Christ's kingdom. S. G. DeGraaf makes the same connection between Solomon's kingdom and the kingdom of Christ. He writes: 'This wonderful kingdom of peace was a foreshadowing of a still more glorious Kingdom of peace that Christ would establish one day.'[1]

2. The visit of the Queen of Sheba to hear the wisdom of Solomon has long been regarded as a picture of the sinner coming to Christ. The Lord Jesus himself used the visit of the queen to convey to the Pharisees the nature of a true response to himself (Matt. 12:42).

3. It cannot be stressed too strongly that Solomon's temple was designed by God himself to portray in advance the redeeming work of the Lord Jesus Christ. This connection is plainly set forth by the author of Hebrews. He tells his readers that Christ himself is both the sacrificing priest and the sacrifice offered by the priest. As the high priest entered the Most Holy Place once a year to make atonement for the sins of his people, so Christ entered 'the Most Holy

Place once for all, having obtained eternal redemption' (Heb. 9:12). A little later he adds: 'For Christ has not entered the holy places made with hands, which are copies of the true, but into heaven itself, now to appear in the presence of God for us...' (Heb. 9:24).

4. The preaching of the prophets during this era also served as a reminder of the coming of Christ (see Isa. 53).

DISCUSS IT

QUESTIONS FOR DISCUSSION

1. The division of Solomon's kingdom testifies to the ruin that comes when we do not guard our hearts against evil (11:4). Read the following: Deuteronomy 26:16; 1 Kings 2:4; Proverbs 3:5; 4:23; Matthew 22:37; Ephesians 6:6; 1 Peter 3:15. What are we to do with our hearts?

2. The glory of Solomon's kingdom prefigured Christ's kingdom. What are some of the qualities of the latter? — John 18:36-37; Romans 14:17; Ephesians 5:5; 2 Peter 1:11; Revelation 11:15. How does one gain access into this kingdom? — John 3:1-8; Luke 22:29; 1 Thessalonians 2:12. How important is Christ's kingdom? — Matthew 6:33.

THE GUIDE

CHAPTER TWELVE

THE SECOND
BOOK OF KINGS

2 KINGS

THE SECOND BOOK OF KINGS

Introduction

INTRODUCTION

2 Kings is the book of downfalls. In chapter seventeen, the northern kingdom (Israel) is taken captive by the Assyrians. In chapter twenty-five, the southern kingdom (Judah) is taken captive by the Babylonians. The former took place in 722 B.C., the latter in 586 B.C.

The reason for these downfalls is not hard to find. Each of the two kingdoms cast off all regard for the laws of God and gave themselves over to sin. After years of warning both kingdoms through the prophets, the Lord finally brought judgement upon them. The dominant theme in 2 Kings is, then, that disobedience brings disaster, or, as one commentator put it: 'Wilful sin brings a woeful end.'[1]

Authorship and purpose

Since 2 Kings was originally the second half of one book, the comments about the authorship and purpose of 1 Kings apply here.

Structure

1. Events in the northern kingdom — mainly about the kings of Israel and the prophet Elisha (1:1 - 10:36)
2. Events in both kingdoms — mainly about the kings of Israel and Judah (11:1 - 17:41)
3. Events in the southern kingdom (18:1 - 25:30)

Overview

Events in the northern kingdom (1:1 - 10:36)

2 Kings opens with Ahaziah, son of Ahab, on the throne of Israel and with Elijah still conducting his prophetic ministry. The focus shifts very rapidly. Ahaziah dies and is succeeded by Jehoram (1:17-18), and Elijah is miraculously transported into heaven and succeeded by Elisha (2:1-18).

The ministry of Elisha was quite different from Elijah's. The latter's ministry was one of judgement, while the former's revealed God's compassion. This should not be construed to mean that Elisha's ministry was superior to Elijah's. Both men were called of God to be prophets and both fulfilled the Lord's purpose for their lives.

Elisha's ministry was also distinguished by the following miracles:

1. purifying bad water (2:19-22)
2. increasing the widow's oil (4:1-7)
3. raising the Shunammite's son from the dead (4:8-37)

4. purifying the poisonous pot of stew (4:38-41)
5. feeding one hundred men (4:42-44)
6. healing Naaman of leprosy (5:1-27)
7. causing the lost axehead to float (6:1-7)
8. blinding Syria's army (6:18-23)

Elisha was so closely associated with the miraculous that one took place in connection with his bones! (13:20-21).

During Elisha's long ministry four kings reigned in Israel: Jehoram, Jehu, Jehoahaz, Jehoash or Joash. All of these were evil kings who continued to lead their nation away from God and into idolatry.

Events in both kingdoms (11:1 - 17:41)

This section alternates between events in Israel and Judah and ends with the former being taken captive by the Assyrians. During the 250 years of her existence (after the division), Israel was ruled by nineteen kings, all of whom were evil. These kings came from seven families. In addition to Elijah and Elisha, the kingdom of Israel was also blessed with the ministries of the following well-known prophets: Amos, Hosea, Jonah.

The seventeenth chapter of 2 Kings, one of the saddest in all the Bible, contains a powerful explanation of Israel's downfall (17:5-23).

TEACHING

Events in the southern kingdom (18:1 - 25:30)

The kingdom of Judah survived her sister kingdom by 136 years. One of the reasons Judah enjoyed this extended period of time was that from time to time she had good kings who led her back to God. Judah lasted 390 years after the division and was ruled by twenty kings, all from the same family — David's.

The following reigned in Judah during the period covered by 2 Kings: Jehoram, Ahaziah, Athaliah (queen), Joash, Amaziah, Azariah (Uzziah), Jotham, Ahaz, Hezekiah, Manasseh, Amon, Josiah, Jehoahaz, Jehoiakim, Jehoiachin, Zedekiah.

The following prophets ministered to Judah during these years: Obadiah, Joel, Isaiah, Micah, Nahum, Habakkuk, Zephaniah, Jeremiah. Ezekiel and Daniel ministered during the captivity while Haggai, Zechariah and Malachi conducted their prophetic ministries during or after the people of God were released from captivity.

Major themes

The same themes that dominate 1 Kings may also be found in 2 Kings: the importance of obedience to God, the faithfulness of God to his promises, the grace and kindness of God (see notes on 1 Kings).

Both 1 and 2 Kings underscore the dreadful nature of sin and how seriously God takes it. They also teach the sombre reality of God's judgement. God sometimes patiently endures the disobedience of his people for a very long time, but he will not always endure it. Disobedience will eventually bring judgement. God's judgement is usually slow in arriving but is severe when it does arrive.

While echoing these themes, 2 Kings makes a unique contribution by stressing the compassion of God for human need and suffering. This is a powerful emphasis in the ministry of Elisha.

Anticipations of Christ

While it contains much that is very serious and sobering, 2 Kings is also a book of hope. We should never forget that it was written to help future generations. The author knew the people of God would not be in captivity for ever. It was vital, therefore, for those who returned to their homeland to be reminded of why this terrible episode in the life of the nation occurred and of how important it was for them to remain true to the Lord.

The period of captivity no doubt caused many to think the promises of God had failed. In particular it seemed that his promises to David, namely, that the Messiah would spring from the line of David, had come crashing to the ground. It is not by mistake that the author closes 2 Kings with a descendant of David not only surviving, but being treated kindly in Babylon (25:27-30).

God's promises had not failed. The Christ would still come from David's line.

Still another anticipation of Christ that may be found in 2 Kings is in the ministry of the prophets. We do not have the preaching of these men recorded in 2 Kings, but we do have it in the books of prophecy (e.g. Isaiah, Jeremiah). Much of their preaching looked towards the coming of the Messiah. There is no better example of this than Isaiah's prophecy of the death of the Messiah (see Isaiah 53).

QUESTIONS FOR DISCUSSION

1. *Elisha's ministry was characterized by compassion. For whom does Christ have compassion? — Matthew 11:28-30; Mark 9:20-22; 10:17-22; Luke 7:13-14; Hebrews 2:17-18.*

2. *Temporal judgements, such as the captivities experienced by both Israel and Judah, remind us of final judgement. Do believers in Christ have anything to fear about that day? — Matthew 25:21,34; John 5:24,29; Romans 2:6,10; 1 Corinthians 4:5; 2 Thessalonians 1:7-10; 2 Timothy 4:8-10; 2 Peter 3:13-14.*

3. *The book of 2 Kings closes on a note of hope for the future. What kind of hope does the Christian have? — 2 Thessalonians 2:16; Titus 2:13; Hebrews 6:19; 1 Peter 1:3.*

CHAPTER THIRTEEN

THE FIRST AND SECOND BOOKS OF CHRONICLES

BIBLE BOOK

THE FIRST AND SECOND BOOKS OF CHRONICLES

Introduction

INTRODUCTION

The books of 1 and 2 Chronicles are the third set of 'double' books in the Old Testament. As is the case with the books of Samuel and Kings, they were originally one.

These books, as their name implies, were intended to 'chronicle'. Their title in the Hebrew language meant 'The Words of the Days', that is, 'The Account or Events of the Days'.

Generally supposed to have been written by Ezra the scribe, these books are concerned with the house of David. After presenting a lengthy genealogy and briefly disposing of the reign of Israel's first king, Saul, the author quickly shifts the focus to David and his descendants and leaves it there.

Purpose

1 and 2 Chronicles were written after the people of Judah returned from their seventy years of captivity in Babylon. They came back to find a

very distressing situation. Their homeland was nothing at all like what it had once been. There was no
descendant of David sitting on the throne. There was
no wall around the city of Jerusalem. There was no
temple in Jerusalem. The author of 1 and 2 Chronicles
wrote to remind these people of their rich spiritual
heritage and to encourage them to renewed faithfulness to God.

Comparison to 2 Samuel and to 1 and 2 Kings

The subject matter of 1 Chronicles roughly parallels
that of 2 Samuel in that it primarily focuses on the reign
of David over all Israel. 2 Chronicles, on the other hand,
finds its parallel in 1 and 2 Kings with the exception
noted above, namely, 2 Chronicles deals only with the
kingdom of Judah and the descendants of David.

While 1 and 2 Chronicles cover the same historical
periods as 2 Samuel and 1 and 2 Kings, it is not mere
repetition. Approximately fifty-five per cent of the
material in 1 and 2 Chronicles is not found in 2 Samuel
or 1 and 2 Kings.

Structure

1. Introduction: genealogies from Adam to Saul
   (1 Chron. 1:1 - 9:44)
2. The tragic end of Saul's reign (1 Chron. 10:1-14)

3. The reign of David (1 Chron. 11:1 - 29:30)
4. The reign of Solomon (2 Chron. 1:1 - 9:31)
5. The kingdom of Judah — division through captivity (2 Chron. 10:1 - 26:23)

Overview

Introduction: genealogies from Adam to Saul (1 Chron. 1:1 - 9:44)

1 Chronicles begins with a genealogy that traces God's redemptive purpose in the nation of Israel. John MacArthur notes: 'This genealogical listing is unique to the purposes of "the chronicler" and is not intended to necessarily be ... exact...' R. C. Sproul writes: 'An essential purpose of the extensive genealogies is to establish that the returned exiles are the legitimate continuation of God's elect people... Their responsibility for obeying is established by their designation as God's elect people.'

The tragic end of Saul's reign (1 Chron. 10:1-14)

After establishing the legitimacy of the returned exiles, the author turns his attention to presenting the monarchy as God's ideal for them. He quickly dispenses with Saul, who was made king because of the people's sinful desire to be like other nations (1 Sam. 8:1-9).

The reign of David (1 Chron. 11:1 - 29:30)

David is presented as the model king for the people of God. While admitting David's faults (1 Chron. 13:7-11; 21:1-7), the chronicler focuses on his tremendous successes (1 Chron. 11:1 - 16:42; 18:1 - 21:30) and on his extensive preparations for the building of the temple (1 Chron. 17:1-27; 22:1 - 29:20).

The reign of Solomon (2 Chron. 1:1 - 9:31)

Solomon, David's successor, led the nation to unprecedented glory and splendour. His primary accomplishment, the building of the temple, is a central theme of 2 Chronicles.

The kingdom of Judah — division through captivity (2 Chron. 10:1 - 26:23)

After Solomon's death the kingdom was divided into two parts with the kingdom of Judah continuing to be ruled by the descendants of David. The chronicler focuses his attention almost entirely on the nation of Judah with only an occasional mention of the rival kingdom of Israel. He records the twenty kings who reigned from the death of Solomon to the captivity in Babylon. He clearly attributes the captivity to the massive idolatry of the people (2 Chron. 36:14) and to their refusal to heed the prophets (2 Chron. 36:16).

After seventy years of captivity in Babylon the people were released by a proclamation of King Cyrus

(2 Chron. 36:22-23). Now back in their homeland, it was up to them to remember God's dealings with their nation and to conduct themselves
according to his laws.

Major themes

1. The blessings of God upon his people when
   they and their king walked in obedience to
   him (as evidenced by the reign of David and
   the early reign of Solomon); and the judgement of God when they failed to do so (2
   Chron. 15:2).

2. The faithfulness of God to his people and his
   promises. Although the people of Judah fell
   into grievous and prolonged sin, the Lord did
   not completely cast them off. He not only
   brought them out of their captivity in Babylon
   but through the Chronicles encouraged them
   to believe that his promises were still intact.
   Their sin had not revoked his election. They
   were still his people (demonstrated by the genealogy). Their sin had not nullified his promises. While there was no descendant of David
   on the throne, the line of David had been preserved, that line from which the Messiah was
   to come.

TEACHING

3. In addition to the above themes, we find 2 Chronicles emphasizing five major periods of revival: under Asa (ch. 15), Jehoshaphat (ch. 20), Joash (chs. 23-24), Hezekiah (chs. 29-31), and Josiah (ch. 35). 2 Chronicles also places a very powerful emphasis on the heart. The Lord watches the heart (2 Chron. 16:9), desires wholeheartedness (15:12,15; 16:9; 19:9; 22:9; 31:21; 34:31) and despises half-heartedness (25:2), hard-heartedness (36:13), and pride of heart (25:19; 26:16; 32:25-26). It is necessary, therefore, for the people of God to 'set' or 'prepare' their hearts (12:14; 19:3; 20:33; 30:18-19).

Anticipations of Christ

Many of the same anticipations of Christ in the books of the Kings apply here as well:

1. The reigns of David and Solomon picture the reign of Christ.
2. The promise to David of a descendant that would reign for ever is a prophecy of the coming of Christ.
3. The temple foreshadows the work of Christ. He is both the High Priest and the sacrifice. He is the meeting place of God and men.

DISCUSS IT

1. *Most of 1 Chronicles is devoted to the reign of King David. Read Simon Peter's sermon in Acts 2:14-36. What prophecies of Christ did Simon Peter find in the writings of David?*

2. *2 Chronicles is a book of revivals. Isaiah 64 provides a wonderful example of yearning for revival. What specific petitions does it contain?*

CHAPTER FOURTEEN

THE BOOKS OF EZRA AND NEHEMIAH

BIBLE BOOK

THE BOOKS OF EZRA AND NEHEMIAH

Introduction

The books of Ezra and Nehemiah deal with the 'post-exilic' period, that is, with that time after the Jews were in captivity in Babylon. This period began in 538 B.C. with the decree of King Cyrus of Persia. The books have traditionally been considered to be authored by the men whose names they bear.

EZRA

Structure

1. The first return to Jerusalem (1:1 - 2:70)
2. The rebuilding of the temple (3:1 - 6:22)
3. The second return to Jerusalem (7:1 - 8:36)
4. The reformation of the people (9:1 - 10:44)

Overview

The first return to Jerusalem (1:1 - 2:70)

In 539 B.C. Babylon was overthrown by the Persians. In 538 B.C. King Cyrus issued a decree that allowed the Jews who had been in captivity in Babylon to return to their homeland. Only 50,000 out of perhaps two or three million decided to take advantage of the decree. The others had grown comfortable in Babylon.

Zerubbabel, whose name means 'descended of Babylon', was a direct descendant of David. He led the tiny remnant back to Jerusalem. Once there, he restored the altar and religious feasts and then began work on the temple.

The rebuilding of the temple (3:1 - 6:22)

The foundation of the temple was laid in 536 B.C., but opposition from outsiders (5:13-17) and the people's interest in their own affairs (Hag. 1:4) soon caused work to cease. From 534 to 520 no work was done. As a result of the ministries of the prophets Haggai and Zechariah, work resumed in 520 and the project was finally complete in 516.

The second return to Jerusalem (7:1 - 8:36)

After being given permission by King Artaxerxes I, Ezra returned to Jerusalem in 458 B.C. with a much smaller group of Jews consisting of less than two thousand.

The reformation of the people (9:1 - 10:44)

Upon his return Ezra discovered that the people had already drifted into violating God's laws. He offered

one of the greatest prayers in the Bible (9:5-15) and led the people into genuine repentance.

NEHEMIAH

Nehemiah led a final group back to Jerusalem in 445 B.C. There he and Ezra formed a wonderful team with Nehemiah serving as the political leader who guided the people in reconstruction, and Ezra serving as the religious leader who brought spiritual renewal.

Structure

1. Reconstruction of the wall (1:1 - 7:73)
2. Renewal of the people (8:1 - 13:31)

Overview

Reconstruction of the wall (1:1 - 7:73)

Nehemiah was serving as a cupbearer to King Artaxerxes in Persia (2:1) when a delegation arrived from Jerusalem to inform him of the desperate conditions there (1:1-3). Nehemiah receives permission from the king to return to his homeland.

Nehemiah returned for the specific purpose of leading the people to rebuild the wall of

TEACHING

Jerusalem. He challenges the people to 'rise up and build' (2:18) and receives a great response. The work had no sooner got underway than fierce opposition arose (4:1 - 6:14), but Nehemiah and the people persevere and complete the project (6:15-19).

Renewal of the people (8:1 - 13:31)

With the wall finished, Nehemiah turned his attention to an even greater task, bringing into existence a godly community. He formed a plan and enlisted Ezra to carry it out (8:1 - 10:39). The people responded in a marvellous way, but the reformation was short-lived. Nehemiah, who returned to Persia in 432 B.C., was compelled to return to Jerusalem in 425 to again bring reformation to the people (13:1-31).

Major themes of Ezra and Nehemiah

The major theme that emerges from these books is quite obvious: God keeps his word. He promised that the people of Judah would be released from their captivity in Babylon and restored to their homeland. These books document that return.

Another important emphasis in these books is God's use of human instruments to accomplish his purpose. In its introduction to the book of Ezra, the *New Geneva Study Bible* documents this point: 'Cyrus issued his decree because the Lord had moved his spirit (1:1). Those who returned came back because the Lord had moved their spirits (1:5). Ezra succeeded because the good hand of God was upon him (7:9). Artaxerxes supported the work of rebuilding because the Lord had put it in his spirit (7:27). Human beings acted freely and responsibly under the providence of God to bring His plans to fruition...'

Yet another theme is the importance of reading God's Word in order to perform his will. Spiritual renewal came to the people as Ezra read from 'the Book of the Law of Moses' (Nehemiah 8:1).

Finally, we see in these books the sufficiency of God's grace for those who attempt to do his will. The Jews who returned to Jerusalem encountered many harsh difficulties and unrelenting opposition, but God enabled them to face all these things.

Ezra and Nehemiah and God's plan of redemption

The books of Ezra and Nehemiah contain a most encouraging message. When the people of God were carried into captivity by Babylon, it appeared that the promises of God could not possibly be fulfilled. There appeared to be no chance that there would continue to be a Jewish people, much less a Messiah descending from David.

The return of the Jews to Jerusalem showed that God's promises were still intact. The very fact that the first return was led by a descendant of David, Zerubbabel, must have spoken volumes to the returning captives. After all their nation had been through, they had even more reason to look forward in complete confidence to the coming of the Messiah.

QUESTIONS FOR DISCUSSION

1. *The book of Ezra records two groups of Jews returning to their homeland from Babylon. What do these returns tell us about the faithfulness of God to his promises? Can you think of other scriptural examples of God's faithfulness? These returns were made possible by the decree of King Cyrus, a pagan ruler. Read Proverbs 21:1. What does it tell us about the Lord's control over kings?*

2. *Nehemiah details the spiritual renewal that took place as Ezra and his assistants helped the people understand God's Word (8:1-12). Read Psalm 119. How many times does this psalm connect spiritual renewal with God's Word?*

CHAPTER FIFTEEN

THE BOOK OF ESTHER

ESTHER

THE BOOK OF ESTHER

Introduction

INTRODUCTION

The book of Esther records events in Persia during the reign of Xerxes (also known as Ahasuerus). Xerxes reigned in Persia from 486 to 465 B.C. During the years of his reign, the Jews who returned to Jerusalem under Zerubbabel were working to rebuild their homeland. It is very important to remember that only a comparatively small number of Jews returned to their land after Cyrus' decree. Most of them stayed in the land of their captivity, and among them were Esther and her cousin Mordecai.

Authorship and date

The author of Esther is unknown. The exact date of the writing of the book is generally thought to be after the death of Xerxes, and many think the book was written around 400 B.C.

Purpose

Esther was written to show that God had not forgotten those of his people who were away from their homeland. Although they were in a foreign land, he was with them and sufficient for them. This book powerfully makes this point without mentioning the name of God at all (the only book of the Bible not to do so). Matthew Henry observes: 'If the name of God is not here, His finger is.'

Structure

The book of Esther is built around a scheme hatched by the evil Haman.

1. The scheme of evil anticipated (1:1 - 2:23)
2. The scheme of evil formulated (3:1 - 4:17)
3. The scheme of evil frustrated (5:1 - 9:17)
4. The defeat of evil celebrated (9:18 - 10:3)

Overview

The scheme of evil anticipated (1:1 - 2:23)

The book of Esther begins with Queen Vashti refusing to obey the order of the king to appear at a feast before his drunken guests (1:10-12). Her refusal led to her

being deposed (1:13-22) and to an extensive search for a successor. The search culminated in Esther, a Jew, being selected. Upon the advice of her cousin Mordecai, who 'took her as his own daughter' after the death of her parents (2:7), Esther did not reveal her nationality (2:10).

Shortly after Esther's selection, Mordecai, who seems to have held some position at the palace (2:5,19,21), discovered an assassination plot against the king. Through Esther he informed the king, and the conspirators were hanged (2:21-23).

The scheme of evil formulated (3:1 - 4:17)

At this point a very evil man, Haman, enters the story. He is promoted to a position of great authority, second only to the king (3:1). Along with his promotion, the king unwisely commanded that all his servants bow and pay homage when Haman came along. Because Mordecai refused to do this, Haman was enraged (3:2-5).

The depth of Haman's evil is evident in the scheme he hatched for dealing with Mordecai. Without mentioning Mordecai at all, Haman convinced the king that all the Jews posed a threat to him and his kingdom, and that they should all be eliminated. The king issued a decree that set a date for his subjects to kill the Jews and take their possessions (3:8-15), a decree that struck his citizens as being very strange (3:15).

TEACHING

The scheme of evil frustrated (5:1 - 9:17)

Haman's vile scheme created great distress among the Jews and caused Mordecai to take action. He pleaded with Esther to go uninvited before the king on behalf of her people. This was a risky act (4:11), but Esther was persuaded by Mordecai's piercing question: 'Who knows whether you have come to the kingdom for such a time as this?' (4:14).

Although he had not called for her, the king welcomed Esther (5:2). Instead of blurting out the plight of her people, Esther invited the king and Haman to a banquet that she had prepared (5:4). At the banquet Esther assured the king that she would let her petition be known if he and Haman would come to yet another banquet on the next day (5:6-8).

While Haman awaited the next day, he was so filled with hatred toward Mordecai that he decided to have gallows built to hang him (5:9-14). He was in for two great surprises. The king, having been reminded of Mordecai's discovery of the assassination plot, called Haman in to ask what should be done for a man who should be honoured by the king. Haman, supposing that he would be the man, suggested that such a man be led around the city on the king's horse by one of the king's princes, and this prince should proclaim: 'Thus shall it be done to the man whom the king delights to honor!' (6:1-9). Immediately the king commanded that Haman do this very thing for none other than Mordecai! (6:10-11).

Before Haman could get over the humiliation of leading Mordecai through the city, it was time to go to

Esther's banquet. There Esther revealed her nationality and Haman's scheme, and the king commanded that Haman be hanged on the gallows he had built for Mordecai (7:1-10).

The death of Haman did not, however, end the threat to the Jews. The king's decree against them could not be revoked, but another decree could be written as long as it did not reverse the previous decree (8:7-8). Mordecai, who had been promoted to Haman's position, solved the Jews' dilemma by writing a decree that allowed them to defend themselves against any attackers (8:11).

The defeat of evil celebrated (9:18 - 10:3)

Mordecai's new decree not only led to the Jews being spared (9:5-6), but also to the institution of a feast as a memorial to their deliverance (9:20-23,26).

Major themes

Some of Esther's major themes are as follows:

1. God's concern for his people even while they were in a foreign land.
2. God's use of human instruments to achieve his purpose.
3. God's ability to overrule human wickedness and to bring good out of it (e.g. the wickedness

that caused Vashti to be deposed brought Esther to
the throne).

4. God's sovereign control of human events. Esther was
   indeed brought to the kingdom for that time (4:14).

God's plan of redemption

The book of Esther reveals yet another of Satan's attempts to destroy the Jewish people and thus defeat
the promise of God to send the Messiah. But God preserved his people and kept his promise.

QUESTIONS FOR DISCUSSION

1. *Queen Vashti's emphatic 'No!' does not stand alone in
   Scripture. Read Genesis 14:21-24; 37:1-22; Ruth 1:14-
   18; 1 Samuel 24:1-22; 26:1-25; Daniel 1:8-21; 6:1-9;
   Hebrews 11:24-26. To what did the saints of God say
   'No' in these passages?*

2. *God did not forsake his people even while they were in
   Persia. Can God's people today be assured of God's
   ongoing presence in every situation and circumstance?
   Read Deuteronomy 31:6; Isaiah 43:1-5; Matthew 28:18-
   20; Hebrews 13:5.*

CHAPTER SIXTEEN

THE BOOK OF JOB

JOB

THE BOOK OF JOB

Introduction

INTRODUCTION

The book of Job brings us to another major division of the Old Testament, the books of poetry. With these books we move away from the emphasis on the national to the personal.

There is much about the book of Job that we do not know. The author and the date of the book are unknown. We also know very little about Job himself. The opening verse tells us that he lived in the land of Uz (1:1), but we cannot say with any degree of certainty when he lived, although many scholars think he was a contemporary of Abraham because of the patriarchal flavour of the book.

Purpose

The book of Job has always carried a lot of appeal because it deals with a matter of intense interest, namely, the suffering of the righteous. We would all like the book to give us a full and complete answer to the question of the suffering of the righteous, but it does not. Its great lesson is the importance of trusting God even when we do not understand what he is doing in our lives. It has been suggested that the book of Job is essentially a detailed illustration of Romans 8:28.

In other words, the book of Job teaches us to trust God's heart even when we cannot trace his hand.

Structure

1. The calamity section (1:1 - 2:13)
2. The counselling section (3:1 - 37:24)
   a. Three cycles of discourses between Job and his friends (3:1 - 31:40)
   b. The Elihu discourse (32:1 - 37:24)
3. The confrontation section — God confronts Job (38:1 - 42:17)

Overview

The calamity section (1:1 - 2:13)

The book begins with a description of Job's righteous character and his tremendous wealth (1:1-5). From there the author shifts rapidly to a scene in heaven. Satan approaches God with the suggestion that Job is righteous only because the Lord has been good to him (1:9-10) and that Job would change abruptly if his circumstances changed from prosperity to adversity (1:11). The

Lord gives permission to Satan to take away all Job's children and his possessions (1:12), which Satan quickly does (1:13-19). While Job deeply lamented his losses, he did not turn against God (1:20-22).

Satan then returned to the Lord to suggest that Job would forfeit his righteousness if physical suffering were inflicted upon him (2:1-6). God again grants Satan permission and Job is visited with painful boils (2:7-8); but Job still refused to curse God.

The counselling section (3:1 - 37:24)

At this point we enter the major section of the book, in which Job's friends gather around to offer him counsel. This portion of the book, as indicated in the structure, consists of two major parts: the three cycles of discourses between Job and his friends (3:1 - 31:40) and the Elihu discourse (32:1 - 37:24).

After an opening lament from Job (3:1-26), the three cycles of discourses run as follows:

1st cycle:　Eliphaz and Job (4:1 - 7:21); Bildad and Job (8:1 - 10:22); Zophar and Job (11:1 - 14:22)

2nd cycle:　Eliphaz and Job (15:1 - 17:16); Bildad and Job (18:1 - 19:29); Zophar and Job (20:1 - 21:34)

3rd cycle: Eliphaz and Job (22:1 - 24:25); Bildad and
            Job (25:1 - 31:40)

Eliphaz, the first of Job's friends to speak, seems to have
been the oldest and most profound. He seems to have
been 'experience-oriented'. He had a vision and assumed
that it made his viewpoint beyond dispute (4:12-16).

Bildad spoke as a scholar who reflected the teaching of a long line of ancestors, and he urged Job to draw
comfort from the same source (8:8).

Zophar is referred to by one commentator as 'one of
those tiresome people — probably just out of college!
— who knows everything!' and says he would be 'high
on the list of those without whom we could happily
live if we never saw them again'.[1]

Other than their willingness to come to Job in his
suffering, there is not much to commend in Eliphaz,
Bildad and Zophar. They attempted to help Job understand his suffering, but he called them 'miserable com-
forters' (16:2), and accused them of speaking 'words of
wind' (16:3).

These three men stand as lasting reminders of the
need to handle suffering friends with great care and to
refrain from giving quick and easy solutions to very
complex and trying problems. Perhaps the most important thing we learn from these men is to speak little
and listen much in our dealings with those stricken by
calamity.

A fourth friend, Elihu, appears to have arrived later
to offer a discourse on the majesty and justice of God

(32:1-37:24). It should be noted that no word of rebuke is offered to Elihu in the book of Job and that God himself speaks immediately after him.

The confrontation section — God confronts Job (38:1 - 42:17)

The book closes with God speaking to Job about his majesty and greatness, and rebuking him for thinking that God owed him some sort of explanation.

Essentially, God said: 'I am God, and you are Job. Trust me!' Job responded to God by confessing that God can do what he pleases (42:1-3) and by repenting of thinking that he could govern the world better than God (42:6). After this, the Lord rebuked Eliphaz, Bildad and Zophar (42:7-9) and restored Job to health and fortune (42:10-17).

Major themes

1. Life in this world is just part of reality. The *MacArthur Study Bible* notes: 'There are matters going on in heaven that believers know nothing about...'[2]
2. Even the most godly suffer. We must, therefore, refrain from pronouncing on someone's spiritual condition when we see them suffering. One can be immensely prosperous and

not be right with God. One can be right with God
and have great adversity.

3. Those who know the Lord should not concern themselves with why they have difficulties but rather with
drawing near to God.

God's plan of redemption

We should remember that while Job was not part of
the nation of Israel (in all likelihood he pre-dated the
beginning of the nation), he did know about the promise that had been given to Adam and Eve of a coming
Messiah and reflects faith in it. The major expression
of Job's faith in that promise is found in these words:

> For I know that my Redeemer lives,
> And He shall stand at last on the earth;
> And after my skin is destroyed, this I know,
> That in my flesh I shall see God,
> Whom I shall see for myself,
> And my eyes shall behold, and not another
>   (19:25-27).

QUESTIONS FOR DISCUSSION

*1. Satan is a real and powerful spiritual being. How did he
become the adversary of God? (Isa. 14:12-15). What is
his final destination? (Rev. 20:7-10).*

DISCUSS IT

2. *Is suffering the common lot of God's people? Read Philippians 1:29-30; 2 Timothy 3:12. What truths soften the experience of suffering for the child of God? Read Romans 8:28; 2 Corinthians 4:8-18; James 1:2-18; 1 Peter 3:13-22.*

CHAPTER SEVENTEEN

THE BOOK OF PSALMS

PSALMS

BIBLE BOOK

THE BOOK OF PSALMS

Introduction

INTRODUCTION

The name 'Psalms' means 'songs'. It is taken from the Greek translation of the Old Testament, which used the title 'Psalmoi'.

The book of Psalms, the largest in the Bible, may very well be the best-loved book of the Bible. John R. W. Stott explains this appeal by saying: 'The reason why Christian people are drawn to the psalms is that they speak the universal language of the human soul... Whatever our spiritual mood may be, there is sure to be a psalm which reflects it — whether triumph or defeat, excitement or depression, joy or sorrow, praise or penitence, wonder or anger.'[1]

While this explains the appeal of the psalms, we should not think the psalmists wrote from an unhealthy self-absorption. They wrote to express praise and worship to God whom they recognized as their Creator and Sustainer. Henrietta C. Mears writes: 'The psalms magnify and praise the Lord, exalt His attributes, His names, His word, and His goodness. Every human experience is related to Him.'[2]

Authorship and date

The psalms are associated with David because he wrote most of them, as the following numerical breakdown indicates:

David — 73 (3-9; 11-32; 34-41; 41-65; 68-70; 86; 101; 103; 108-110; 122; 124; 131; 133; 138-145)
Asaph — 12 (50; 73-83)
Descendants of Korah — 10 (42; 44-49; 84-85; 87)
Solomon — 2 (72; 127)
Ethan — 1 (89)
Heman — 1 (88)
Moses — 1 (90)
Anonymous — 50 (many of these may also have been written by David; see, for example, Acts 4:25)

The psalms were composed over a period of approximately 900 years, from Moses (1410 B.C.) to the post-exilic period (see Ps. 126).

Structure

The book of Psalms consists of five books:

1. Book I – 1-41 (41 psalms)
2. Book II – 42-72 (31 psalms)
3. Book III – 73-89 (17 psalms)
4. Book IV – 90-106 (17 psalms)
5. Book V – 107-150 (44 psalms)

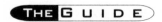

Types of Psalms

1. Psalms of lament

These psalms express the desire for God to deliver. They are divided into individual laments (3-7; 12; 13; 22; 25-28; 35; 38-40; 42-44; 51; 54-57) and communal laments (59-61; 63; 64; 69-71; 74; 79; 80; 83; 85; 86; 88; 90).

2. Psalms of thanksgiving

These psalms thank God for the blessings he has bestowed and express confidence that he will bestow further blessings. They may also be divided into individual and communal. The psalms of thanksgiving are: 8; 18; 19; 29; 30; 32-34; 36; 40; 41; 66; 103-106; 111; 113; 116; 117; 124; 129; 135; 136; 138; 139; 146-148; 150.

3. Enthronement psalms

These psalms describe God's sovereign rule over all (47; 93; 96-99).

4. Pilgrimage psalms

These psalms were sung by pilgrims travelling to Jerusalem for the great annual feasts held there (43; 46; 48; 84; 87; 120-134).

5. *Royal psalms*

These pertain to the king as God's chosen ruler (2; 18; 20; 21; 45; 72; 89; 101; 110; 132; 144).

6. *Wisdom psalms*

These offer the reader instruction and guidance for living righteously (1; 37; 119).

7. *Imprecatory psalms*

These psalms ask God to judge his enemies (7; 35; 40; 55; 58; 59; 69; 109; 137; 139; 144).

The imprecatory psalms deserve special mention because they seem to be cruel. *The Open Bible* offers this explanation: 'Although some of them seem unreasonably harsh, a few things should be kept in mind: (1) they call for divine justice rather than human vengeance; (2) they ask for God to punish the wicked and thus vindicate his righteousness; (3) they condemn sin (in Hebrew thinking no sharp distinction exists between a sinner and his sin); and (4) even Jesus calls down a curse on several cities and tells His disciples to curse cities that do not receive the gospel (Matt. 10:14,15).'[3]

8. *Confidence psalms or psalms of trust*

These psalms express faith in God's care for and guidance of his people (4; 11; 16; 23; 27; 62; 125; 131).

Messianic psalms

Many of the above psalms may also be classi-fied as 'messianic'. This means they look beyond the immediate circumstances in which the author found himself, to the person and work of the Lord Jesus Christ. The enthronement psalms, for example, may be taken as pictures of the kingly reign of Christ. The principal messianic psalms are: 2; 8; 16; 20; 21; 22; 23; 24; 31; 35; 40; 41; 45; 50; 55; 61; 68; 69; 72; 89; 96; 97; 98; 102; 109; 110; 118; 132. *The Open Bible* gives the following helpful list of specific messianic references in Psalms:

	Prophecy	*Fulfilment*
2:7	God will declare him to be his Son.	Matt. 3:17
8:6	All things will be put under his feet.	Heb. 2:8
16:10	He will be resurrected from the dead.	Mark 16:6,7
22:1	God will forsake him in his hour of need.	Matt.27:46
22:7-8	He will be scorned and mocked.	Luke 23:35
22:16	His hands and feet will be pierced.	John 20:25, 27
22:18	Others will gamble for his clothes.	Matt. 27:35-36

TEACHING

34:20	Not one of his bones will be broken.	John 19:32-36
35:11	He will be accused by false witnesses.	Mark 14:57
35:19	He will be hated without a cause.	John 15:25
40:7,8	He will come to do God's will.	Heb. 10:7
41:9	He will be betrayed by a friend.	Luke 22:47
45:6	His throne will be for ever.	Heb. 1:8
68:18	He will ascend to God's right hand.	Mark 16:19
69:9	Zeal for God's house will consume him.	John 2:17
69:21	He will be given vinegar and gall to drink.	Matt. 27:34
109:4	He will pray for his enemies.	Luke 23:34
109:8	His betrayer's office will be fulfilled by another.	Acts 1:20
110:1	His enemies will be made subject to him.	Matt. 22:44
110:4	He will be a priest like Melchizedek.	Heb. 5:6
118:22	He will be the chief cornerstone.	Matt. 21:42
118:26	He will come in the name of the Lord.	Matt. 21:9[4]

Conclusion

The psalms teach us to be much occupied with God. This means we are to treasure his Word, to delight in his worship, to reflect on his glorious attributes, to rehearse his great acts in history, to trust in his care, to glory in his gospel and to anticipate his final victory. The more occupied with God we are, the more strength we find for living.

DISCUSS IT

QUESTIONS FOR DISCUSSION

1. The imprecatory psalms bring before us the solemn reality of the wrath of God. Read John 3:36; 2 Thessalonians 1:3-10. Who will be the recipients of God's wrath in eternity? Who alone can save us from God's wrath? — Romans 5:9; 1 Thessalonians 1:9-10.

2. In Psalm 23, the psalmist delighted in the Lord as his shepherd. Read John 10:11-30. What did Jesus promise to do for his sheep?

3. Read Psalm 119. How do we show we value the Word of God? Give special attention to the following verses: 1,2,3,6,7,11,13,14-16.

CHAPTER EIGHTEEN

THE BOOK OF PROVERBS

PROVERBS

BIBLE BOOK

THE BOOK OF PROVERBS

Introduction

INTRODUCTION

The word 'proverb' is a combination of two Latin words: '*pro*' and '*verba*'. The former means 'for' and the latter means 'words'. A proverb is, therefore, 'for or in the place of words'. It is something of a verbal shortcut. It is a brief saying instead of many words. William Hendriksen defines proverbs as 'tersely expressed deductions from daily experience'.[1] Another commentator says a proverb is 'a shrewd concentration of truth', and goes on to say, 'Its purpose is not to explain a matter but to give pointed expression to it.'[2]

In short, a proverb may be considered to be a short expression drawn from long experiences.

Purpose and authorship

The book of Proverbs is exactly what its title suggests. It is a collection of proverbs or sayings. It is likely that the people of Israel made use of proverbs from the earliest years of their history.

Part of their covenant relationship with God was to see to it that their children had proper religious training (Deut. 6:4-9). In the process of this training, proverbs came to be used.

King Solomon, who wrote 3000 proverbs during his lifetime (1 Kings 4:32), was the primary author and collector of these proverbs (1:1), but others contributed proverbs which he used (30:1; 31:1), and King Hezekiah was responsible for adding some of Solomon's proverbs (25:1 - 29:27). When King Solomon came to the throne of Israel, there were already a great number of these proverbs in existence. He gathered them into a collection and added several hundred of his own. Some think he also set up special schools for the religious training of young men and that his collection of proverbs was used in them.

Structure

1. Instructions (1:8 - 9:18)
2. Sayings (10:1 - 22:16; 25:1 - 29:27)
3. Admonitions (22:17 - 24:22)

The instructions consist primarily of long poems that usually begin with the direct address 'my son' and contain commands or prohibitions with reasons attached. The sayings are characterized by extreme brevity. They are straightforward insights about reality and leave readers to draw their own conclusions. The admonitions are shorter forms of instructions.

TEACHING

Another way to structure the book is as follows:

1. Proverbs of Solomon for the young (1:1 - 9:18)
2. Proverbs of Solomon for all (10:1 - 22:16)
3. The words of the wise (22:17 - 24:34)
4. Proverbs of Solomon collected by Hezekiah (25:1 - 29:27)
5. The words of Agur and Lemuel (30:1 - 31:31)

Major themes

Proverbs is a book about wisdom. The wise person has understanding, discernment, perception and insight. The Hebrew words from which these are translated appear sixty-six times in the book. The wise person reflects a good understanding in the following areas:

1. *a proper relationship with the Lord*

   a. he fears the Lord (1:7; 3:7). Fearing the Lord means standing in awe of his person and dreading his displeasure.
   b. he rests in knowing the Lord is in control (16:1-3)
   c. he trusts the Lord for direction (3:5-6)
   d. he accepts his discipline (3:11-12)

2. *speech* (17:28; 18:7-8; 18:21)

The wise person knows the value of silence (17:28), the harm of gossip (18:7-8), and the tremendous power of the tongue (18:21).

3. *labour* (20:4,13)

The wise person observes the lazy person. He notes both his flimsy excuses for not working and his miserable end (20:4), and disciplines himself to work (20:13). He functions on the basis of principle rather than of feeling.

4. *truth* (22:20-21)

The wise person recognizes the character of truth, namely, that it is both excellent and certain. Its excellence arises from what it produces, that is, great comfort, pleasure and satisfaction. Its certainty stems from the fact that it is God's truth and nothing can change it. The wise person also recognizes his personal responsibility to absorb the truth (1:8; 2:1-5; 4:1,10-22; 5:1; 7:1) and to share the truth (22:21).

5. *self-control in eating and drinking* (23:20-21)

6. *good companions* (13:20; 14:7; 22:24-25; 24:21)

Three words are used for those whom the righteous person seeks to avoid: *kesil*, *'ewil* and *nabal*. The *kesil* is one who makes choices on the basis of what provides immediate pleasure, choices that ultimately lead to ruin. The *'ewil* is worse than the *kesil*. He is one who is spiritually and morally stupid. The *nabal* is one who is insensitive to the Lord, morally apathetic, and rejects what is reasonable.

7. *family relationships* (30:17; 31:10,25-30)

The wise child respects his parents (30:17; 31:28), and the wise husband respects his wife (31:10,25-30). Wise parents discipline their children (13:24; 19:18; 22:6,15; 23:13-14; 29:15,17).

8. *contentment with possessions* (28:6,22)

The wise person is more concerned about what is in his eye than how much is in his hand. He knows that filling the hand with goods often requires 'an evil eye', that is, an eye filled with greed. The wise person desires to have a pure eye, even if it means an empty hand.

9. *control of anger* (26:21; 29:22)

Among the many enemies constantly seeking entrance into the human spirit are anger (29:22) and contentiousness (26:21). The former is the inward feeling that often finds expression in the latter. The person who nurses anger and resentment will eventually find himself unable to get along with others. He will constantly be starting quarrels or entering into quarrels that have been started by others.

10. *humility* (27:1-2; 29:23)

The proud person takes life for granted and presumes he will always occupy the same position or one greater. He fails to see the uncertainty and unpredictability of life (27:1). He also doesn't hesitate to tell others about himself (27:2). The humble person, on the other hand, knows he lives by the grace of God and must take nothing for granted. He also leaves it to others to praise him.

11. *compassion for enemies and for the poor* (25:21-22; 28:27)

12. *sexual morality* (2:16-19; 5:3-6; 6:20-35; 7:6-27)

The above topics and references are only a sample of teaching on how the wise person lives. There are also teachings about friends, finances, honesty in business, vengeance, and many other matters. There is also teaching about the results of living wisely and unwisely.

Proverbs and God's plan of redemption

The purpose of God's plan of redemption is to save sinners from their sin. The book of Proverbs reflects the

DISCUSS IT

kind of life the child of God is to live. Many Bible students regard the speech of wisdom (8:1-36) as the Messiah himself speaking. The Lord Jesus Christ is the wisdom of God (1 Cor. 1:30).

QUESTIONS FOR DISCUSSION

1. Read the New Testament book of James. What themes does it share with the book of Proverbs?

2. Read Genesis 13:1-13 and Judges 16:1-22 to discover some Bible characters who failed to govern their lives with the wisdom commended by the book of Proverbs. Can you think of others?

THE GUIDE

CHAPTER NINETEEN

THE BOOKS OF ECCLESIASTES AND SONG OF SOLOMON

BIBLE BOOK

THE BOOKS OF ECCLESIASTES AND SONG OF SOLOMON

Introduction

This study brings us to the two most difficult and unused books of the Bible. Candour compels many Christians to say with Stuart Olyott: 'For years I had a Bible with two books missing. They had been printed all right, but I never read them. I could not make head nor tail of them, and so ignored them. For all practical purposes they did not exist.'[1]

ECCLESIASTES

Authorship

The author of Ecclesiastes identifies himself as 'the Preacher, the son of David, king in Jerusalem'. While all the descendants of David were in a sense his sons, and while many of them were kings, there can be little doubt that the son who wrote this book was Solomon. Warren Wiersbe rightly points out: 'As the wisest, wealthiest, and most powerful man of his day, Solomon certainly had the opportunity and resources to do the things mentioned in Ecclesiastes.'[2]

Purpose

This book was written to deal with a very significant and pressing question, namely, is life worth living? Solomon's treatment of this question troubles many. He seems in places to contradict and challenge other scriptural teachings. The problems are resolved when we keep in mind that Solomon is concerned to show his readers life from two viewpoints. The first is the viewpoint of the natural person, the one who lives 'under the sun' (occurring twenty-nine times). This is the person who is earthbound in his perspective. He is the one for whom life in this world is the sum of reality, the one who views life apart from God. The conclusion of this man is 'All is vanity' (occurring thirty-nine times), that is, there is no real meaning to be found in this life.

The other perspective is that of the person who knows and worships God and believes the truths God has revealed. Life has meaning for this person. (The name of God appears forty times.)

Throughout the book Solomon alternates between these two viewpoints so that he can show, in the words of Irving Jensen, 'the futility of pursuing materialistic, earthly goals as an end in themselves, and ... point to God as the source of all that is truly good'.[3]

Structure

1. Introduction (1:1-11)
2. Sermon one (1:12 - 3:15)
3. Sermon two (3:16 - 5:20)
4. Sermon three (6:1 - 8:13)
5. Sermon four (8:14 - 12:7)
6. Conclusion or summary (12:8-14)

Major themes

Intellect (1:12-18), pleasure (2:1-11), success (2:12-17), labour (2:18-23), popularity (4:13-16), wealth (4:8; 5:10-13) and children (6:3-6) are some of the main things to which people look for meaning and satisfaction in life. While these may very well provide temporary satisfaction, they cannot finally satisfy. True satisfaction can only be found in fearing God and keeping his commandments (12:13-14). The sooner one begins to serve God the more opportunities he has to find deep peace and satisfaction (12:1).

God's plan of redemption

Satisfaction is found in God and God alone, and there is only way to God, that is, through faith in his Son, Jesus Christ. Christ is the 'one

Shepherd' (12:11) who gives abundant life to his sheep (John 10:9-10).

THE SONG OF SOLOMON

Authorship

The Song of Solomon, also known as the Song of Songs and Canticles (derived from the Latin word meaning 'songs'), was written by Solomon.

Overview

The Song of Solomon is Solomon's account of falling in love and marrying a shepherdess known as the Shulamite (probably indicating that she was from the area of Shunem). Stuart Olyott offers this summary of the book:

> King Solomon had a vineyard in the hill country of Ephraim, about fifty miles north of Jerusalem, which he let out to keepers (8:11). These keepers consisted of a mother, her two sons and their younger sister, the Shulamite (1:6; 6:13; 8:8). The Shulamite was the 'Cinderella' of the family, naturally beautiful, but unnoticed (1:5). Very probably her brothers were half-brothers (1:6). They made her work very hard in the vineyard, so that

TEACHING

she had virtually no time to care for her personal appearance (1:6). She pruned the vines, set the traps for the little foxes, kept the flocks, and was out in the open so much that she became extremely sunburned (2:15; 1:8,5).

One day, disguised, Solomon arrived at the vineyard and showed an interest in her (1:6). She took him to be a shepherd and asked about his flocks (1:7). He answered evasively, but also spoke loving words to her and promised her rich gifts in the future (1:8-11). He won her heart and left with the promise that he would return some day. That night she dreamed of him, and sometimes thought that he was near (3:1). Finally he *did* return, in all his kingly splendour, and took her to be his bride (3:6-7).[4]

Structure

1. The courtship (1:1 - 3:5) — the main speaker is the Shulamite who recalls the events that led to her wedding.
2. The wedding (3:6 - 5:1) — the main speaker is Solomon who praises his bride.
3. The marriage (5:2 - 8:14)
   a. An experience of alienation (5:2 - 6:3) — the main speaker is the bride.

b. The renewal of love (6:4 - 8:4) — the main speaker is Solomon.

c. The experience of settled devotion (8:5-14) — the husband and wife speak equally.

This structure moves us through three stages of love: love awakened, love tested and love triumphant.

The Song of Solomon and Christ

While the Song of Solomon certainly has to do with romantic love between husband and wife, Christians down through the centuries have also been able to see it as a picture of Christ's love for his church. We do not strain the meaning of the Song by viewing it in this way. The Old Testament consistently speaks of God's love for Israel in terms of a husband's love for his wife (Ps. 45; Hos. 1-2), and the New Testament speaks of Christ's love for his church in the same way (Eph. 5:22-33).

Believers who view the Song in this manner do so because of these words regarding the Lord Jesus: 'And beginning at Moses and all the Prophets, he expounded to them in all the Scriptures the things concerning himself' (Luke 24:27). If the Lord Jesus is in 'all the Scriptures', he must certainly be in the Song of Solomon.

Interpreting the Song of Solomon in such a way makes it a very searching book. Is our love for Christ comparable to what we find expressed here? Every Christian loves Christ, but love can grow cold (Rev. 2:4).

The question is not whether Christians love Christ, but rather whether they love him to the degree they should, that is, with the same fervent, passionate love that the Shulamite had for Solomon.

QUESTIONS FOR DISCUSSION

1. Who in the New Testament was like the preacher in Ecclesiastes, one who tried many things before finding satisfaction? Where did this New Testament character finally find peace? Read Philippians 3:1-16.

2. Read Ephesians 5:22-33. Who is the standard for how husbands are to love their wives? Who is the bride of Christ? Read Revelation 19:1-10. What is the event called when Christ takes his bride unto himself?

DISCUSS IT

CHAPTER TWENTY

THE BOOK OF ISAIAH

ISAIAH

BIBLE BOOK

THE BOOK OF ISAIAH

Introduction

INTRODUCTION

This study brings us to the last of the major divisions of the Old Testament: the prophets. This category of books is subdivided into the major prophets and the minor prophets. The division is based solely on the size of the respective books.

Isaiah was a prophet to the kingdom of Judah. Born in Jerusalem around 760 B.C., he was called to be a prophet at the end of Uzziah's reign (6:1-10) and continued through the reigns of Jotham, Ahaz and Hezekiah. It is thought by many that he lived into the very evil reign of Manasseh (circa 695-642 B.C.) during which he was executed by being 'sawn in two' (Heb. 11:37).

The years of Isaiah's life and ministry were tumultuous and threatening. Assyria was the major world power at the time, and Judah's sister kingdom, Israel, fell to her during Isaiah's ministry. Judah herself came perilously close to falling to Assyria during the reign of Hezekiah but was miraculously spared (36:1 - 37:38). Isaiah died well before his nation was carried away captive by the Babylonians in 586 B.C., but he prophesied both the captivity (39:1-8) and the decree of Cyrus that would allow his people to return to their homeland (44:28 - 45:1).

Purpose and structure

The prophecy of Isaiah, written by the prophet himself, falls into two major divisions. The first part was written to declare God's forthcoming judgement upon the sins of the people. The second part was designed to bring comfort to those who were to be carried into captivity. A large proportion of the second part brings comfort by pointing to the coming of their Messiah.

1. Present prophecies (1:1 - 39:8) — Isaiah prophesies judgement to his own generation
   a. prophecies of judgement on Judah (1:1 - 12:6) — this section contains the call of Isaiah (6:1-13) and the 'Book of Immanuel' (7:1 - 12:6), in which Isaiah prophesies the coming Christ
   b. prophecies of judgement on surrounding nations (13:1 - 24:23)
   c. hymns and prophecies calling for trust in God (25:1 - 35:10)
   d. historical events (36:1 - 39:8)
2. Future prophecies (40:1 - 66:24) — Isaiah prophesies comfort to a new generation
   a. The coming deliverance (40:1 - 48:22)
   b. The coming Messiah (49:1 - 57:21)
   c. The glorious future (58:1 - 66:24)

TEACHING

Special features

1. Isaiah is quoted directly in the New Testament at least sixty-five times, far more than any other Old Testament prophet. In these quotations, the prophet is called by name more than twenty times.
2. Isaiah is noted for the richness of his vocabulary. He uses a total of 2,186 different words in his prophecy, while the psalmists use 2,170 words, Jeremiah 1,653, and Ezekiel 1,535.
3. Some have noted that Isaiah is something of a miniature Bible. The Bible consists of sixty-six books, which are divided into the thirty-nine books of the Old Testament and the twenty-seven books of the New Testament. Isaiah consists of sixty-six chapters, which are divided into two parts, the first consisting of thirty-nine chapters and the second of twenty-seven.
4. Isaiah had two sons whom he named Maher-shalal-hash-baz ('speedy is the prey') and Shear-jashub ('a remnant shall return'). These two names illustrated the two parts of Isaiah's message.

Major themes

1. The majesty and glory of God (6:1-5; 40:12-31)
2. God's demand for reality in religion and justice in society (1:1-23; 3:13-23)

3. The importance of trusting God's wisdom rather than human wisdom (25:9; 26:3-9; 30:1-3,18; 31:1-3)
4. The folly of idolatry (40:21-29; 44:9-20)
5. The concern and compassion of God for his people (40:11; 41:10; 43:2-4)

Anticipations of Christ

The prophecy of Isaiah is well known for its many prophecies of the Lord Jesus Christ. *The Open Bible* is certainly correct in saying of Isaiah: 'His messianic prophecies are clearer and more explicit than those in any other Old Testament book.'[1]

These are some of Isaiah's prophecies with references from the New Testament that assert their fulfilment:

Prophecy	*Fulfilment*
7:14	Matthew 1:22-23
9:1-2	Matthew 4:12-16
9:6	Luke 2:11; Ephesians 2:14-18
11:1	Luke 3:23,32; Acts 13:22-23
11:2	Luke 3:22
28:16	1 Peter 2:4-6
40:3-5	Matthew 3:1-3
42:1-4	Matthew 12:15-21
42:6	Luke 2:29-32
50:6	Matthew 26:67; 27:26,30
52:14	Philippians 2:7-11
61:1-2	Luke 4:17-19,21

There is no greater example of fulfilment of Isaiah's prophecies than that of Isaiah 53. If the promises of the cross in the prophets may be considered a mountain range, this chapter is the Mount Everest of that range. Eight of its twelve verses are quoted in the New Testament in connection with the Lord Jesus Christ (1,4,5,6,7,8,9,11).

This much loved chapter lends itself to a threefold division: the life of Christ (vv. 1-3), his death (vv. 4-10), and the results of his death (vv. 10-12). The major part of it, however, is devoted to his death on the cross.

The writers of the New Testament vigorously affirm that each of the following seven prophecies found its fulfilment in Christ:

1. He would be wounded for our transgressions, bruised for our iniquities and receive 'stripes' for our healing (v. 5) — 1 Peter 2:24
2. He would be silent before his accusers (v. 7) — Matthew 26:63
3. He would be buried in a rich man's tomb (v. 9) — Matthew 27:57-60
4. He would be innocent of any wrong-doing (v. 9) — 1 Peter 2:22
5. He would be numbered with transgressors (v. 12) — Mark 15:28
6. He would make intercession for transgressors (v. 12) — Luke 23:34

7. All of these things would be in keeping with God's plan: God would smite him (v. 4), lay our iniquities upon him (v. 6), and bruise him (v. 10) — John 5:30; 8:42; 18:11.

Why did Christ have to suffer such untold agony and anguish on the cross? Isaiah's repeated use of the pronoun 'our' and the preposition 'for' tells us that Jesus would not die for his own sins, but rather for the sins of his people. It was 'our griefs' and 'our sorrows' that he carried with him to the cross. And it was 'for our transgressions', 'for our iniquities' and 'for our peace' that he died (53:4-5). It tells us that the Christ would not die as others. His death would have the significance no other death in all of human history would have. It was to be a death for others, a death in which he took the place of others and bore their penalty.

Isaiah's amazingly detailed description also unfolds the spirit with which Jesus would suffer (53:7). Christ went to the cross, not with a grudging obedience that could not find any way to get around it, but with a glad and ready willingness. During his public ministry, he constantly emphasized that he had come to do the Father's will, and that will carried him all the way to the cross. Even when the cross was scant hours away, he was able to say to the Father: '...your will be done' (Matt. 26:42).

In addition to those prophecies already fulfilled, Isaiah includes prophecies that await complete and final fulfilment at the end of time: 11:6-9; 65:17-25. The

fact that so many of Isaiah's prophecies have been fulfilled should cause us to have no doubts at all about these being fulfilled as well.

DISCUSS IT

QUESTIONS FOR DISCUSSION

1. Read Deuteronomy 13:1-3; Jeremiah 23:16-32. What are some of the characteristics of false prophets?

2. Comfort is a major theme of Isaiah 40-66. Read 2 Corinthians 1:3-4; John 14:16-18,26; 15:26 - 16:15; Romans 15:4; 2 Corinthians 7:6. What are some of the sources of the Christian's comfort?

CHAPTER
TWENTY-ONE

THE BOOKS OF JEREMIAH AND LAMENTATIONS

BIBLE BOOK

THE BOOKS OF JEREMIAH AND LAMENTATIONS

JEREMIAH

Introduction

INTRODUCTION

The book of Jeremiah records the ministry of the prophet whose name it bears. The book was compiled by Baruch the scribe who copied the prophet's messages (36:4,32; 45:1).

Jeremiah, the son of the priest Hilkiah, was born in Anathoth, just two miles north of Jerusalem. His ministry fell into two major sections. From 626 to 586 B.C., he warned the nation of Judah of God's impending judgement, a warning that was realized in 586 when the Babylonians finally crushed Judah and carried most of her citizens into captivity. From 586 to approximately 575, Jeremiah ministered to those who were not taken captive by Babylon.

No one has ever been called to minister in more difficult situations than Jeremiah. The first part of his ministry was conducted with the knowledge that judgement was about to fall. The second part was conducted in the midst of the devastation and heartache created by that judgement.

Purpose

Jeremiah's primary purpose was to call the people of Judah to return to the Lord. The word 'return' occurs forty-seven times in the book. Jeremiah could see the judgement of God rumbling towards Judah because of the sins of the people. The only way the people could avert judgement was to break decisively with their sins and return wholeheartedly to the Lord.

Jeremiah is known as 'the weeping prophet' (9:1; 13:17; 14:17) because he was heartbroken over his people's unwillingness to repent and because of the devastating judgement that lay ahead.

Structure

1. Jeremiah's call (1:1-17)
2. Jeremiah's ministry to Judah (2:1 - 45:5)
    a. Condemnation (2:1 - 25:38)
    b. Confrontation (26:1 - 29:32)
    c. Consolation (30:1 - 33:26)
    d. Consummation (34:1 - 45:5)
3. Jeremiah's messages to other nations (46:1 - 51:64)
4. The overthrow of Jerusalem (52:1-34)

Overview

In its introduction to the prophecy of Jeremiah, *The Open Bible* gives this admirable summary:

Jeremiah is a record of the ministry of one of Judah's greatest prophets during its darkest days. He is called as a prophet during the reign of Josiah, the last of Judah's good kings. But even Josiah's well-intentioned reforms cannot stem the tide of apostasy. The downhill slide of the nation continues virtually unabated through a succession of four godless kings during Jeremiah's ministry. The people wallow in apostasy and idolatry and grow even more treacherous than Israel was before its captivity (3:11). They pervert the worship of the true God and give themselves over to spiritual and moral decay. Because they refuse to repent or even listen to God's prophet, the divine cure requires radical surgery. Jeremiah proclaims an approaching avalanche of judgement. Babylon will be God's instrument of judgement, and this book refers to that nation 164 times, more references than the rest of the Bible.

Jeremiah faithfully proclaims the divine condemnation of rebellious Judah for forty years and is rewarded with opposition, beatings, isolations, and imprisonment. His sympathy and sensitivity cause him to grieve over the rebelliousness and imminent doom of his nation. He often desires to resign from his prophetic office because of the harshness of his message and his reception, but he perseveres to Judah's bitter end.[1]

Major themes

In addition to the theme noted above, returning to the Lord, the following should be noted:

1. The character of God. Because God is all-knowing, he is aware of human sin. Because God is holy, he will not tolerate it for ever. Because God is sovereign, he can do something about sin.
2. The nature of real repentance (94:1-4)
3. The folly of relying on mere religious rituals to please God (The Temple Sermon — 7:1 - 8:3)
4. The reality and danger of false prophets (23:9-40; 28:1-17)
5. The indestructibility of God's Word (36:1-32)
6. The inevitability of suffering for those who dare to stand for God in evil times.
7. The grace of God. Although the people sinned so grievously and were facing captivity, the Lord did not abandon them.

Anticipations of Christ

The prophecy of Jeremiah includes powerful passages on the coming Messiah. The Messiah is referred to as 'a Branch of righteousness' (33:15) and 'THE LORD OUR RIGHTEOUSNESS' (33:16).

The greatest of the messianic passages is found in Jeremiah's 'Book of Consolation' (chs. 30-33), in which he presents the new covenant. In this covenant, the people of God would have the laws of God written on their hearts and would enjoy a close, intimate relationship with God. They would also rejoice in widespread knowledge of God. All of these blessings were to flow from the free pardon of their sins (31:31-34). These blessings were to be secured by the Lord Jesus Christ.

LAMENTATIONS

Lamentations, as its title indicates, is a book of grief and mourning. It was written after the people of Judah fell under the judgement predicted by Jeremiah and other faithful prophets. The Babylonians had invaded the land, destroyed Jerusalem, and carried off a great number of the people.

TEACHING

Jeremiah, the author, was one of a tiny remnant left in the land. In this book he expresses the pain and anguish of all his people and his own deep sorrow.

Lamentations consists of five poems, corresponding to the five chapters in our Bibles. Each poem is in the form of an acrostic (running successively through the letters of the Hebrew alphabet). Each of the four outer poems (chs. 1,2,4,5) consists of twenty-two verses, with each verse beginning with one of the twenty-two letters of the Hebrew alphabet. The central poem (ch. 3) consists of sixty-six verses, but is also an acrostic with each triplet of verses beginning with one of the twenty-two letters of the Hebrew alphabet.

Each of the five poems has its own theme:

chapter 1 — Jerusalem's desolation
chapter 2 — Jehovah's anger
chapter 3 — Jeremiah's grief and consolation
chapter 4 — Jerusalem's siege
chapter 5 — Jerusalem's prayer

The devastating experience of the city of Jerusalem is representative of what the Lord Jesus Christ himself would endure in the process of his redeeming work. He would be, as Jerusalem was:

1. the afflicted of the Lord (1:12)
2. despised by his enemies (2:15-16)
3. a derision among the people (3:14)
4. smitten and insulted (3:30)

DISCUSS IT

1. *Jeremiah was 'the weeping prophet'. On what occasions did Jesus weep? Read Luke 19:28-44; John 11:17-37; Hebrews 5:5-8 (cf. Matt. 26:36-38).*

2. *Read Hebrews 8:1-12; 10:16-17. How do the blessings of the new covenant come to us?*

CHAPTER
TWENTY-TWO

THE BOOK OF
EZEKIEL

EZEKIEL

BIBLE BOOK

THE BOOK OF EZEKIEL

Introduction

INTRODUCTION

Ezekiel was a prophet to the people of Judah during their years of captivity in Babylon. This captivity came about in three stages. The first occurred in 605 B.C. when Daniel and his friends were taken. The second occurred in 597 B.C. when ten thousand more of Judah's citizens, including Ezekiel, were taken. Then in 586 B.C. Nebuchadnezzar and his forces dealt the final blow to Judah by destroying the city of Jerusalem and carrying away even more captives. Ezekiel seems to have begun his prophetic ministry around 592 B.C. and continued it until the year 570.

Purpose

Ezekiel's primary purpose was threefold: (1) to show his fellow-captives the reasons for the plight of their nation; (2) to reveal God's forthcoming judgement on other nations; and (3) to declare the glorious future that lay ahead.

Structure

1. Ezekiel's call (1:1 - 3:27)
2. Ezekiel's message of judgement on Judah (4:1 - 24:27)
3. Ezekiel's message of judgement on Judah's neighbours (25:1 - 32:32)
4. Ezekiel's message of hope and restoration (33:1 - 48:35)

The last three points of this structure reflect the three major divisions of Ezekiel's ministry. During the early years (592-587), before Jerusalem's destruction, he was compelled to convince his captives that there was no hope for immediate deliverance. During the siege of Jerusalem (586), Ezekiel warned her neighbours not to gloat over her judgement because they were destined to face the same destruction. After Jerusalem's fall (585-570), Ezekiel turned to the theme of hope and restoration for the nation.

Special features

1. Ezekiel's name means 'God strengthens'. This was a most fitting name. The great need of Ezekiel and his fellow-captives was to be strengthened by God.
2. Ezekiel, like Jeremiah, was the son of a priest (1:3; 40:46; 44:15).

TEACHING

3. No prophetic book contains more dates than Ezekiel. There are twelve such references (1:1,2; 8:1; 20:1; 24:1; 26:1; 29:1; 30:20; 31:1; 32:1,17; 40:1).

4. Ezekiel uses a distinctive style. Irving L. Jensen writes: 'Ezekiel's style is very lofty. He has brought prose and poetry together in one masterpiece. The book abounds with visions, parables, allegories, apocalyptic imagery, and various symbolic acts.'[1]

5. Ezekiel is known as 'The Prophet of Visions'. The following are the visions recorded in his book:

   • the Lord (1:4-28)
   • the scroll (2:9 - 3:3)
   • the plain (3:22-23)
   • the abominations in the temple (8:1-18)
   • the slain inhabitants of Jerusalem (9:1-11)
   • Jerusalem destroyed by fire (10:1-22)
   • the Lord departing from Jerusalem (11:1-25)
   • the dry bones (37:1-10)
   • the new temple (40:1 - 48:35)

6. Ezekiel is also known for his symbolic actions, that is, seemingly strange deeds which God commanded him to perform so that his message might be pressed more indelibly on his hearers.

Sign	Teaching	Passage
1. Sign of the Brick	Jerusalem's siege and fall	4:1-3
2. Sign of the Prophet's Posture	Discomforts of captivity	4:4-8
3. Sign of Famine	Deprivations of captivity	4:9-17
4. Sign of the Knife and Razor	Utter destruction of the city	5:1-17
5. Sign of House Moving	Removal to another land	12:1-7, 17-20
6. Sign of the Sharpened Sword	Judgement imminent	21:1-17
7. Sign of Nebuchad-nezzar's Sword	Babylon the captor	21:18-23
8. Sign of the Smelting Furnace	Judgement and purging	22:17-31
9. Sign of Ezekiel's Wife's Death	Blessings forfeited	24:15-27
10. Sign of the Two Sticks	Reunion of Israel and Judah	37:15-17[2]

Major themes

1. *The attributes of God.* Ezekiel emphasizes God's glory, sovereignty, name, holiness, justice and mercy. The phrases 'glory of the God of Israel' and 'glory of the Lord' appear eleven times in the first eleven chapters.

The title 'Lord God' appears over two hundred times in the book.

2. *The involvement of God with his people through his prophet*. The phrase 'the word of the Lord came unto me' appears forty-nine times.

3. *Individual responsibility*. The *New Geneva Study Bible* explains this emphasis in this way: 'The Exile had come about in part as a result of the cumulative guilt of generations of Israelites who had lived in rebellion against God and his law. While guilt always has a corporate dimension, Ezekiel, more than any prophet before him, emphasized the individual consequences of disobedience and transgression.'[3]

4. *The danger of false prophets*. Ezekiel warned his fellow-captives about the folly of believing those who preached the captivity would last less than the seventy years that had been prophesied by Jeremiah (Jer. 29).

The best-known chapter

Most Bible students would be quick to name Ezekiel 37 as the one with which they are most familiar. This chapter powerfully drives home the theme of Israel's restoration.

After giving Ezekiel a tour of a valley of dry bones, a tour that impressed the prophet with the number and the extreme dryness of the bones, the Lord posed what would seem to be the most ridiculous question that has ever been asked: 'Son of man, can these bones live?' (v. 3). Ezekiel answered: 'O Lord GOD, you know' (v. 3).

Ezekiel was then given the command to prophesy to the bones. The prophecy met with immediate results: a great shaking, bone joining to bone (v. 7), sinews and flesh covering the bones (v. 8). Then everything came to a stop. Ezekiel had begun with a valley of bones and now he had an army of corpses. The Lord told him to prophesy to the four winds. Immediately breath came into the corpses and they lived (vv. 9-10).

The Lord then gave Ezekiel an explanation for this bizarre experience. That valley full of dry bones was equivalent to the situation Ezekiel's people were in at that time. No one in his right mind would dare suggest that dry bones can live again, and no one seeing Judah's captivity in Babylon would dare suggest that she could live again as a nation. Both situations were equally hopeless, so much so that the nation of Israel was essentially saying, 'Our bones are dry, our hope is lost, and we ourselves are cut off!' (v. 11).

But God specializes in hopeless situations, and he here tells Ezekiel that the seemingly hopeless situation of Judah was going to be reversed. She would be brought out of her grave in Babylon and restored to her land (v. 12).

Anticipations of Christ

The Open Bible says: 'Ezekiel depicts the Messiah as a tender twig that becomes a stately cedar on a lofty mountain... The Messiah is the King who has the right to rule (21:26,27), and he is the true Shepherd who will deliver and feed His flock (34:11-31).'[4]

QUESTIONS FOR DISCUSSION

DISCUSS IT

1. *The seemingly hopeless situation presented in Ezekiel 37 reminds us that nothing is impossible with God. Read Genesis 18:1-15; Jeremiah 32:16-25; Luke 1:26-38; 18:24-27. What are the 'impossible' situations represented in these passages?*

2. *Ezekiel's name, 'God strengthens', must have served as an encouraging reminder to his fellow-captives as they faced the pressures of living in Babylon. Read Psalm 46:1-3; 73:25-26; Isaiah 40:27-31; 41:8-10; 2 Corinthians 12:1-10. Does God provide strength for his people today in their trials and crises? In what situations and trials can God's people count on him providing strength?*

CHAPTER
TWENTY-THREE

THE BOOK OF
DANIEL

DANIEL

BIBLE BOOK

THE BOOK OF DANIEL

Introduction

INTRODUCTION

The prophecy of Daniel, written by Daniel himself, is, like that of Ezekiel, set in the context of the Jews' captivity in Babylon. As noted in the study of Ezekiel, this captivity came about in three stages. Daniel and his friends were taken in the first stage (605 B.C.). While Ezekiel was called to minister to his fellow-captives in Babylon, Daniel was placed in the Babylonian court at the heart of Babylonian culture. There, because of his God-given ability to interpret dreams and his faithfulness, Daniel rose to a position of prominence.

Daniel is one of the greatest men of the Old Testament. He is one of only a few of whom nothing negative was written. He was a man of faith, courage and consistency. His name has become synonymous with standing for convictions and refusing to compromise in the face of tremendous pressure.

Structure

1. Six narratives (1:1 - 6:28)
   a. The king's food (1:1-21)
   b. The king's dream (2:1-49)
   c. The king's image (3:1-30)
   d. The king's second dream (4:1-37)
   e. The handwriting on the wall (5:1-31)
   f. The lion's den (6:1-28)
2. Four visions (7:1 - 12:13)
   a. Four beasts (7:1-28)
   b. The ram and the goat (8:1-27)
   c. The seventy weeks (9:1-27)
   d. The latter days (10:1 - 12:13)

Overview

The six narratives (1:1 - 6:28)

The first six chapters of Daniel show us how Daniel and his friends maintained faithfulness to God in a hostile culture. It is evident from the opening verses that the Babylonians intended to denationalize Daniel and his friends, to strip them of everything Jewish (including their religion), and to make them tools for the government to use in subduing and governing their countrymen more easily. Daniel and his friends did not object totally to the ways of Babylon, but only to those that would cause them to violate the laws of God.

1. chapter 1 — Daniel and his friends refuse to eat food sacrificed to idols
2. chapter 3 — Daniel's friends refuse to grant to Nebuchadnezzar's image the homage that belongs to God alone, and are cast into a furnace
3. chapter 6 — Daniel refuses to obey the king's decree that no one pray to anyone except the king for thirty days. Because of his refusal to comply, Daniel is thrown into the lion's den

The narrative section also features Daniel proclaiming God's truth to pagan kings:

1. chapters 2 and 4 — Daniel interprets dreams for Nebuchadnezzar
2. chapter 5 — Daniel interprets the handwriting on the wall for Belshazzar

The four visions (7:1 - 12:13)

The last half of Daniel (the four visions) brings us to what is known as 'apocalyptic literature', that is, literature that was written to encourage the people of God in times of severe persecution. Stuart Olyott writes of this type of literature: 'The main themes are always the same — the growth of evil, God's care for His people, and the assurance that evil will not finally prevail. The only thing of eternal duration is the kingdom of God.'[1]

1. chapter 7 — *the four beasts*. Daniel sees four empires, one succeeding the other: Babylon, Medo-Persia, Greece and Rome.

2. chapter 8 — *the ram and the goat*. The ram represents the Medo-Persian Empire. Its two horns represent the Medes and Persians merging into one. The goat represents Greece and its great horn Alexander. The four horns represent the generals who became kings after Alexander's kingdom was divided into four parts. The little horn represents Antiochus Epiphanes, who rose from the third empire to rule one of these four parts, namely, the Syrian division. Antiochus Epiphanes also represents the final Antichrist.

3. chapter 9 — *the seventy weeks*. Daniel sees a period of seventy 'sevens' or a period of 490 years which were to unfold in three distinct stages: one of 'seven weeks' (49 years), one of 'sixty-two weeks' (434 years), and one of 'one week' (7 years). The first of these periods was to begin with the command to rebuild the city of Jerusalem. The second was to begin at the end of the first and was to consist of 434 years. These two periods total 483 years. If we accept the first decree of Artaxerxes in 473 to rebuild the city of Jerusalem as the starting point for Daniel's vision and add 483 years, we arrive at the date for Jesus' baptism.

It is obvious that Gabriel was giving Daniel a vision of the coming Messiah. He came on the public stage to perform his public ministry by submitting to baptism. Daniel was given to understand, then, that the Messiah would come on the scene 483 years after the decree to rebuild the city of Jerusalem.

What was the nature of the Messiah's work? Daniel 9:24 says the Messiah would finish transgression, make an end of sin, make reconciliation for iniquity, bring in an everlasting righteousness, seal up the vision (that is, fulfill prophecy), and anoint the Most Holy (that is, enter into heaven itself to make intercession for us — Heb. 9:12,24). Midway through this third week (three and a half years), the Messiah would be 'cut off, but not for himself' (9:26). In other words, he died as predicted by Isaiah, not for his own sins but for the sins of others (Isa. 53:4-6). By his death on the cross, the Lord Jesus caused sacrifice and offerings to cease (9:27). There was no more need of them since he, the perfect sacrifice, had died (think of the rent veil in the temple at the precise moment Jesus died).

It is important to keep in mind that the great purpose behind this vision was to lift Daniel and his people from being overly concerned with the rebuilding of their city and their temple. The real focus of their faith and their real hope was in the coming of Christ.

4. chapters 10-12 — *the latter days*. Daniel sees the coming of the Antichrist (11:36-37, cf. 2 Thess. 2:3-10) and a period of terrible, unprecedented tribulation (12:1). He also sees the

glorious victory that awaits the children of God (12:2-3).

Major teaching

The dominant theme in the book of Daniel is the sovereign rule of God (the name Daniel means 'God rules'). The rule of God means he can and does intervene in the kingdoms of this world (4:17,25,32,34-35). The narrative section of Daniel powerfully drives home this theme. The recurring phrase in this section is 'the God of heaven' (2:19,28,37,44). Because God rules:

1. He can enable his people to stand in the midst of evil times (1:1-21)

2. He gives kingdoms to men and takes them away (2:37; 4:28-33; 5:1-31).

3. He can intervene in the affairs of men at any time (6:27). Examples of this are: God granting dreams to Nebuchadnezzar and interpretations to Daniel, God using miraculous means to deliver his people — the fiery furnace (ch. 3), the handwriting on the wall (ch. 5), and the lion's den (ch. 6).

4. He can promise to 'set up a kingdom which shall never be destroyed', a kingdom that 'shall break in pieces and consume' all other kingdoms and shall 'stand forever' (2:44; 6:26).

DISCUSS IT

The rule of God is still the theme when we come to the four visions of Daniel. These visions show how God's promise to set up his universal and eternal kingdom will be brought to pass. It is all through the work of the Lord Jesus Christ. His work is anticipated in the narrative portion and amplified in the vision portion of Daniel. In the former he, the Messiah, is 'the stone' that was 'cut out of the mountain without hands', the stone that shatters the kingdoms of men (2:45). In the latter, he is 'the Ancient of Days' (7:9-10) and the fulfilment of the Seventy Weeks Vision (9:20-27).

QUESTIONS FOR DISCUSSION

1. Daniel stands as an example of one who is faithful to God. Read the following verses: Psalm 31:23; Proverbs 28:20; Matthew 25:14-23,45-46; Revelation 2:10. What has God promised to his faithful people? Read Psalm 101 to see how David prized faithfulness.

2. Daniel and his friends were 'in' Babylon but not 'of' Babylon. Does the Lord call his people today to be 'in' the world but not 'of' it? Read John 17:6-19. What can you do to keep from being 'of' the world?

THE GUIDE

CHAPTER
TWENTY-FOUR

THE BOOK OF HOSEA

HOSEA

THE BOOK OF HOSEA

Introduction

INTRODUCTION

The prophecy of Hosea brings us to that portion of the Old Testament that we know as 'Minor Prophets'. These twelve books are so designated, not because they are minor in message, but rather because they are small in size.

Hosea ministered to the northern kingdom of Israel immediately before it was carried into captivity by the Assyrians in 722 B.C. His ministry may be placed between the years of 754 and 714 B.C.

Purpose

Hosea was called to minister in terrible times indeed. From the time it split from the house of David, the kingdom of Israel had been involved in idolatrous worship (1 Kings 12:1-33). In addition, Hosea also found social injustice and moral breakdown, which always arise from idolatrous behaviour.

Hosea was called to denounce the idolatry (which amounted to spiritual adultery), to warn of judgement and to call for repentance. Three phrases seem to perfectly summarize his message:

1. 'you have' — indicating the sins Israel had committed
2. 'I will' — occurring fifty-seven times, these words of the Lord warned of the impending judgement
3. 'you may' — even though Israel had grievously sinned, the Lord graciously extended to them the invitation to repent of their sins and return to him.

We should note that Hosea also sounded a note of hope for the people as he promised eventual restoration for the land (14:1-9).

Distinguishing features

1. Hosea is quoted by the New Testament writers more often than any of the other minor prophets — thirty times.

2. Hosea gives insight into the tenderness of God's heart and his longing for his people (11:8-9).

3. Hosea's marriage to Gomer is the vehicle God used to deliver his message against Israel's spiritual adultery.

TEACHING

Structure

Introduction (1:1)
1. The prophet's personal experience (1:2 - 3:5)
2. The application to the nation (4:1 - 12:14)
   a. The controversy of God with his people
      (4:1 - 9:9)
   b. A history of infidelity (9:10 - 12:14)
3. The decision facing Israel (13:1 - 14:9)
   a. Rebellion leading to death (13:1-16)
   b. Repentance leading to life (14:1-9)

Overview

Introduction (1:1)

The prophet's personal experience (1:2 - 3:5). God had entered into a covenant relationship with the nation of Israel. He was committed to love her, protect her and provide for her. She had agree to love, honour and obey him.

For a long time the nation was true to God, but then she began to follow other gods, especially Baal. God called Hosea to provide shock treatment for Israel. He told him to marry 'a wife of harlotry' (1:2). Hosea's marriage was to parallel at every point God's relationship with Israel. God had called the nation out of idolatry to be his wife. Israel had stayed faithful for a while and brought forth spiritual fruit. But then she turned back to idolatry and was now committing spiritual adultery. Hosea was, then, to marry a harlot woman who would be faithful to him and bear him children. But, just like Israel, she would then become unfaithful.

Are we shocked by what God had Hosea do? This was exactly what God intended. He wanted the people of Israel to be shocked by what they had done to him.

God also wanted to deliver a message through the names of Hosea's children (1:4-9):

1. Jezreel — this place, where the evil Jezebel died, was synonymous with judgement
2. Lo-Ruhamah — 'not pitied'. God would cease to show mercy to Israel
3. Lo-Ammi — 'not mine'. God would not acknowledge Israel as his own

The application to the nation (4:1 - 13:16)

The controversy of God with his people (4:1 - 9:9). The Lord's message is presented in terms of a lawsuit. The Lord here deals with the conduct of the people (4:1-3), the character of the religious leaders (4:4-10), the corruption of worship (4:11-19; 8:11-14) and the corruption of the political leaders (7:1-16; 8:8-10).

He also deals in this section with the devastating judgement that was rumbling towards Israel (5:1-15; 8:1-7; 9:1-9) and warns about superficial repentance (6:1-11).

A history of infidelity (9:10 - 12:14). The Lord draws significant names from Israel's past to make her aware of the gravity of her present sin: Baal Peor (9:10-14, cf. Num. 25:1-3), Gilgal (9:15 - 10:8, cf. 1 Sam. 8:7), Gibeah (10:9-15, cf. Judges 19:1 - 21:25). He also mentions Israel's bondage in Egypt (11:1-11) to drive home their sin of forgetfulness, and Jacob (11:12 - 12:14) to remind them of their deceitfulness.

The decision facing Israel (13:1 - 14:1-9)

Rebellion leading to death (13:1-16). There was no other saviour (vv. 4-8) or king (vv. 9-13) for Israel except in God. If Israel refused to recognize this, she would experience severe judgement (vv. 4-16).

Repentance leading to life (14:1-9). The prophecy closes with the Lord issuing a tender appeal for the people to return to him (vv. 1-3) and with the assurance that judgement would not be the final word for Israel, and a glorious future of restoration lay ahead (vv. 4-9).

Anticipations of Christ

Although Hosea was ministering to the nation of Israel, he did not hesitate to point to the house of David and the promises that God had made regarding it, namely the coming of the Messiah, as the true hope for the nation (3:5).

The Gospel of Matthew also sees Jesus' flight into and return from Egypt as a fulfilment of Hosea 11:1.

QUESTIONS FOR DISCUSSION

1. *God's phrase 'I will', so frequently used in Hosea, was often upon the lips of Jesus during his earthly ministry. Read Matthew 11:28-30; 16:13-19; John 6:37,44; 12:30-32; 14:1-3,15-18,21; Revelation 3:20. What does Jesus tell us that he will do for his people?*

2. *Hosea is an appeal to God's people to return from their backsliding. Read Jesus' parable of the prodigal son in Luke 15:11-24. What caused the son to return to his father? What kind of reception did he receive?*

CHAPTER
TWENTY-FIVE

THE BOOKS OF
JOEL AND AMOS

BIBLE BOOK

THE BOOKS OF JOEL AND AMOS

JOEL

Introduction

There is a great deal of debate about the time Joel prophesied to the kingdom of Judah. Some scholars place him among the post-exilic prophets, but most think he ministered about 835 B.C. during the reign of Joash. This date seems preferable over a post-exilic date because Amos, who prophesied around 760 B.C., seems to have borrowed some of Joel's phrases. If this was the case, Joel had to pre-date Amos.

Purpose and theme

While the date of Joel's prophecy can be disputed, his message cannot. It is a clear, ringing call to the people of Judah to repent of their sins and turn back to wholehearted allegiance to the Lord. R. A. Stewart calls Joel 'one of the most disturbing and heart-searching books of the Old Testament'.[1]

Joel uses the phrase 'the day of the Lord' a total of five times in this book (1:15; 2:1,11,31; 3:14). The *Holman Bible Dictionary* defines this day in this way: 'The time when God reveals His sovereignty over human powers and human existence'.[2]

'The day of the Lord' can refer, then, to any day in human history in which God has manifested his sovereignty in an unusual way, and also to that coming day in which his sovereignty over all nations and all creatures will be abundantly plain.

Structure

1. A plea for repentance (1:1 - 2:17)
   a. indications of the need for repentance — past and future calamities (1:1 - 2:11)
   b. the nature of genuine repentance (2:12-17)

2. A promise of blessing (2:18 - 3:21)
   a. A promise to pity (2:18)
   b. A promise to provide food and to remove shame (2:19)
   c. A promise to remove the enemy (2:20)
   d. A promise to restore productivity (2:21-26)
   e. A promise to provide spiritual renewal and vitality (2:27-32)
   f. A promise to judge other nations (3:1-17)
   g. A promise of general blessing (3:18-21)

TEACHING

Overview

Joel prophesied to Judah shortly after the nation had experienced a devastating plague of locusts (1:2-4) and a severe drought (1:10-12,17-20). These terrible plagues pre-figured the even more terrible calamity that lay ahead of Judah, a calamity that would consist of an invading army (2:1-11). Sincere and deep repentance of sin was the only way for the people to avoid this calamity (2:12-17). In addition to removing the threat of judgement, this type of repentance would also open the floodgates of God's blessings upon them (2:18 - 3:21).

Major themes

1. The sovereignty of God over all nature
2. The devastating results of sin
3. The reality and severity of God's judgement

Anticipations of Christ

Joel 2:28-29 are the best-known verses in this little prophecy, mainly because they were quoted by the apostle Peter on the Day of Pentecost. The Spirit of God came in great power on that occasion because the Lord Jesus Christ, now exalted to heaven and at the right hand of God, poured the Spirit out upon his people. The Spirit's presence was the infallible sign of Christ's exaltation, and Christ's exaltation was due to the completion of his redeeming work.

AMOS

Introduction

Amos, whose name means 'burden-bearer', was a herdsman by trade. He was something of an oddity among prophets in that he was called to preach to the kingdom of Israel even though he was a native of Judah. Amos prophesied to Israel during the long reign of Jeroboam II (786-746 B.C.). More specifically, Amos' ministry is to be dated two years before an unusually severe earthquake (1:1). The exact date of this earthquake is not known, but many scholars accept 760 B.C. as the beginning of Amos' ministry, placing the earthquake in 758.

Purpose and theme

Amos was called to warn Israel that the Lord would most certainly send severe judgement upon her if she did not break with her sins. We might state Amos' theme of judgement in this way: because of Israel's sins a time was coming when God would pass *through* them and not *by* them (5:17; 7:8; 8:2).

Structure

1. Sermons (1:2 - 6:14)
   a. Eight 'roars' of judgement (1:2 - 2:16 — key phrase: 'Thus says the LORD')
   b. Three pleas to hear (3:1 - 5:15 — key phrase: 'Hear this word')
2. Visions (7:1 - 9:10 — key phrase: 'Thus the Lord GOD showed me')
   a. The judgements God refused to employ (7:1-6)
   - the locusts (7:1-3)
   - the fire (7:4-6)
   b. The judgements God chose to employ (7:7 - 9:10)
   - the plumb line (7:7-17)
   - the summer fruit (8:1-14)
   - the stricken doorposts (9:1-10)
3. Promises (9:11-15)

Overview

Amos' time was one in which things were going so splendidly that his message of judgement made it appear that he had lost his mind. It was a time of prosperity, stability and flourishing religion (3:12,15; 4:1,4; 5:5,21-23; 6:4,6; 8:3,10). But all was not well with Israel. Corruption, greed, oppression of the poor (2:6; 5:11), religious formalism (5:21), idolatry (4:4), immorality (2:7) and disdain for authority (5:10,12) also flourished.

J. I. Packer writes:

Into this complacent community God dropped a bombshell in the shape of farmer Amos. Amos came storming into Samaria as a prophet of doom for Church and nation. God, he said, was about to judge his people (2:6 - 4:3). The wheel of retribution was already spinning, and would soon go faster. Recent disasters — the drought, the bad harvest, the famine, the epidemic, the earthquake — had shown God's displeasure clearly enough (4:6-11), and these were only a beginning; soon the whole nation would be enslaved and deported (5:27)... Worse still, the streams of revelation were going to dry up. There would be 'a famine of hearing the words of the Lord'.[3]

Major themes

1. The seriousness of sin
2. The coming of judgement
3. The holiness of God
4. The mercy of God

Anticipations of Christ

Amos' stern message of judgement for Israel was tempered with hope. In the closing verses of his prophecy, Amos portrays a glorious future for the people of God. In describing this future, he mentions the king (9:11), the nations (9:12), the earth (9:13), the people (9:14), and the land (9:15).

These promises are of such a nature that they could only be fulfilled by the Lord Jesus Christ himself. Specifically, he is the king from the house of David that would raise it from ruins (9:11).

QUESTIONS FOR DISCUSSION

1. Read Revelation 20:11-15. Is this a 'day of the Lord'? Who will be present? How are they judged? What is their sentence?

2. How does Acts 15:16-17 apply the words of Amos 9:11-12?

CHAPTER
TWENTY-SIX

THE BOOKS OF
OBADIAH
AND JONAH

2

THE BOOKS OF OBADIAH AND JONAH

OBADIAH

Introduction

The book of Obadiah is the shortest in the Old Testament. It reveals nothing about the prophet except his name, which means 'servant of the Lord' or 'worshipper of the Lord'. Thirteen Old Testament men bear the name of Obadiah, and attempts have been made to identify the prophet with one of these, but this is sheer guesswork.

Purpose and theme

The setting of the book of Obadiah is also uncertain. We know it is placed against the backdrop of Judah's neighbouring nation, Edom, participating in an invasion of Judah. Scholars mention the following invasions as possibilities: (1) Egypt under King Shishak (1 Kings 14:25-26); (2) The Philistines and Arabians during the reign of Jehoram (2 Chron. 21:16-17); (3) Israel under King Jehoash (2 Kings 14:2; 2 Chron. 25); (4) The invasion of Babylon that culminated in the collapse of Judah in 586 B.C. (2 Kings 24-25). This invasion seems to be the most likely in view of what one of the psalms has to say about the response of the nation of Edom to it (Ps. 137:7).

Edom's rejoicing over this calamity put the people of Judah in quite a quandary. Why would God bring such severe judgement upon his own people, and seemingly let a nation like Edom get away with their wickedness? The prophecy of Obadiah answers that question in this way — the fact that wicked people *seem* to be getting away with their wickedness doesn't mean they are. No one ever gets away with wickedness. Sooner or later God will step in and balance the books. The *New Geneva Study Bible* says: 'When the church suffers at the hands of God's enemies, she needs to return to the prophecy of Obadiah and renew her faith in the just God revealed there. He cares for His persecuted people, and behind their present circumstances He is always at work for them.'[1]

Structure

1. A word of warning for the people of Edom (vv. 1-16)
2. A word of consolation for the people of God (vv. 17-21)

Major themes

1. God's sovereignty extends even to people who are not his.
2. Pride and cruelty are especially hateful to God.
3. The wicked may gloat over God's people in this world, but a day is coming when he will show that they are his and that they were right to serve him.

Anticipations of Christ

Two of Obadiah's phrases gives us glimpses of Christ: 'on Mount Zion there shall be deliverance' (v. 17) and 'the kingdom shall be the LORD's' (v. 21). Those phrases dealt with the near future for the nation of Judah. She would indeed be delivered from her captivity and restored to her land in such a way that it would be clear that she was really the Lord's kingdom and that he was working on her behalf. But while the primary application of these phrases has to do with Judah of old, it is legitimate to see in them a picture of the far greater deliverance that awaits all the people of God — the deliverance from all sin and sorrow when 'the kingdoms of this world have become the kingdoms of our Lord and of his Christ' (Rev. 11:15).

TEACHING

JONAH

Introduction

The story of Jonah is one of the most familiar in the Bible. We know little about the prophet himself. Verse one tells us he was the son of Amittai. 2 Kings 14:25 places his ministry in Israel during the reign of Jeroboam II and tells us that he was from the village of Gath Hepher.

Purpose and theme

The purpose of the book is very clear, that is, to show that there is a wideness in God's mercy, that while God had chosen Israel as his own, he was not obligated to limit himself to Israel.

Structure

1. God pursues his disobedient prophet (1:1-17)
2. God rescues his disobedient prophet (2:1-10)
3. God uses his obedient prophet (3:1-10)
4. God rebukes his sulking prophet (4:1-11)

Overview

The book opens with Jonah being called by the Lord to go to Nineveh, located on the Tigris River in the

Assyrian Empire, and declare there the impending judgement of God (1:2). Jonah responded by going in the opposite direction. He caught a ship in Joppa (on the Mediterranean coastline of Israel), which was sailing to Tarshish, and which some have identified as Tartessus in southern Spain.

Why did Jonah flee from the Lord? Jonah was well aware that his nation, Israel, had for many years been living in disobedience to the Lord. He must have interpreted his call to preach to Nineveh as an indication that the Lord was about to set unrepentant Israel aside and enter into a covenant relationship with the Ninevites. By fleeing, he thought he could thwart God's plan and thus protect his own nation. Jonah's action was sheer folly. O. Palmer Robertson writes: 'Trying to get away from God is like trying to get away from air.'[2]

God brought Jonah around by first sending a great storm upon the sea (1:4). When the sailors discovered that Jonah was the cause of the storm, they cast him overboard (1:7-15). They undoubtedly thought that would be the end of Jonah, but 'the LORD had prepared a great fish to swallow' the prophet (1:17).

In the belly of the fish, Jonah thoroughly repented of his rebellion (2:1-9), and the Lord delivered him from the fish (2:10). After receiving a second command to preach in Nineveh (3:1-2), Jonah obeyed. His preaching met with great results. The people repented of their sins and the Lord lifted the threat of judgement (3:5-10).

The book closes with Jonah complaining about the Lord showing mercy to Nineveh (4:2), and with the Lord giving the prophet an object lesson. The Lord withered the vine under which Jonah had found relief from the heat, and then asked this question: If it was fitting for Jonah to have pity on the vine was it not more fitting for him, the Lord, to show pity to Nineveh? (4:10-11).

We do not know how Jonah answered that question. Perhaps the book ends with the question hanging so that we will have to answer it ourselves. In short, the option before each child of God is to be like Jonah or to be like Jesus. Jonah grieved over a repentant city that had to be spared, while Jesus grieved over an unrepentant city that had to be judged (Luke 19:41-44).

Other major themes

1. The sovereignty of God over all creation
2. God's willingness to forgive and restore his backslidden people
3. The importance of prompt obedience to the Lord

Anticipations of Christ

While some have questioned whether Jonah could actually have been swallowed by a great fish and live to tell the story, the Lord Jesus Christ accepted the

DISCUSS IT

historicity of the account and used it as a picture of his resurrection from the grave (Matt. 12:39-41). He also used the story of Jonah to rebuke the Pharisees for not heeding his message. The people of Nineveh repented when they heard Jonah's preaching, and the Pharisees had in Jesus 'a greater than Jonah' (Matt. 12:41).

QUESTIONS FOR DISCUSSION

1. *How does God view pride? Read Psalm 18:27; 138:6; Proverbs 8:13; 16:5; 21:4; James 4:6; 1 John 2:16.*

2. *Jonah was correct in saying that God is gracious, merciful, slow to anger and abounding in lovingkindness (4:2). What do we receive from God because he possesses these attributes? Read Ephesians 1:6-7; 2:1-10; Titus 3:1-7; Hebrews 4:14-16; 1 Peter 1:3-5.*

CHAPTER
TWENTY-SEVEN

THE BOOKS OF MICAH AND NAHUM

BIBLE BOOK

THE BOOKS OF MICAH AND NAHUM

MICAH

Introduction

The prophet Micah, whose name means 'who is like God', came from the little town of Moresheth-gath, which was located about twenty-five miles south-west of Jerusalem. He was called to minister to the kingdom of Judah during the reigns of Jotham (739-731 B.C.), Ahaz (731-715 B.C.) and Hezekiah (715-686 B.C.). Micah conducted his ministry at the same time Isaiah was ministering in Judah and Hosea in Israel.

While Micah's ministry was directed to Judah, he also addressed the kingdom of Israel, which fell to the Assyrians during his ministry (722 B.C.).

Purpose and theme

Micah's message emphasizes God's forthcoming judgement and his gracious promise to restore them. Micah presents this message in terms of a controversy between God and his people (1:1). We might say he takes the people of Judah into God's courtroom where God is both the accuser and the judge.

Structure

The prophecy of Micah may be divided into three major sections, each beginning with the word 'hear' (1:2; 3:1; 6:1) and each ending with a note of hope (2:12-13; 5:7-15; 7:18-20).

1. The capital cities are called to hear (1:2 - 2:13)
2. The leaders are called to hear (3:1 - 5:15)
3. The people are called to hear (6:1 - 7:20)

Overview

Judgement always seems to be harsh and unwarranted to us. Sinful men always harbour resentment and suspicion towards God. When he sends good to us we think we deserve more. When he brings evil upon us we think we deserve none. The prophets of God realized this terrible tendency. They always went to great lengths, therefore, to make it clear that God's judgement is not just arbitrarily sent with no rhyme or reason but rather because of sin. In the case of Judah, sin was widespread. It was not a case of just one section of society sinning, both the people and their leaders had abandoned God's principles.

Micah charges the people with idolatry (1:7; 6:16), covetousness (2:2), oppression (2:2) and violence (2:2; 3:10; 6:12; 7:2). He charges the leaders with disregard for justice (3:1-3,9-10), hating good and loving evil (3:2), oppression of the poor (3:2-3), obsession with money (3:11) and with a presumptuous attitude that assumed God would not judge (3:11).

Major themes

The prophecy of Micah emphasizes the same major themes as the other prophets — the holiness and sovereignty of God, the seriousness of sin, the certainty of judgement, and the grace of God that promises restoration. The teaching that separates Micah from the other prophets is his demonstration of the close connection between true religion and ethical behaviour. This is also found in the other prophets, but the classic statement on it belongs to Micah:

> He has shown you, O man, what is good;
> And what does the LORD require of you
> But to do justly,
> To love mercy,
> And to walk humbly with your God?
>
> (6:8).

TEACHING

Anticipations of Christ

In all the minor prophets there is no clearer prophecy
of the Lord Jesus Christ than the one found in Micah
5:2-5. This passage lays out: (1) Bethlehem as the birthplace of the Lord Jesus; (2) the nature of his work, that
is, ruler in Israel (v. 2) and the shepherd of his people
(v. 4); (3) his deity (v. 2).

The closing verses of the prophecy (7:18-20) also
compel us to think of the redeeming work of Christ. It
is because God 'delights in mercy' that he has made a
way for our iniquities to be pardoned and subdued.
That way is his Son, Jesus Christ, who fulfils the promises which God had 'sworn' to the fathers 'from days of
old' (7:20).

NAHUM

Introduction and purpose

Around 760 B.C. God sent the reluctant prophet Jonah
to Nineveh, the capital of the Assyrian Empire, to warn
of his impending judgement. The people of the city
repented and were spared (Jonah 3:1-10).

While that spiritual awakening was deep and real,
it was not long before the Ninevites returned to wickedness. The prophet Nahum was called, then, to do as
Jonah had done, that is, to proclaim the coming destruction of Nineveh. This time there would be no

escape. The cup of iniquity was full. Nahum's prophecy (circa 620 B.C.) was fulfilled in 612 B.C. when Nineveh fell to Babylon.

The name 'Nahum', a shortened version of 'Nehemiah', means 'comfort' or 'consolation'. Nahum's message of judgement on the Ninevites brought comfort to all who lived in mortal dread of their ruthless and brutal practices. For the people of that day to hear the news that Nineveh had fallen would be like the World War II generation hearing that Germany had collapsed.

Structure

1. Nature of Nineveh's judge (1:1-8)
2. Assurance of Nineveh's judgement (1:9-15)
3. Horror of Nineveh's judgement (2:1 - 3:7)
4. Unity with Thebes — No Amon (3:8-11)
5. Manifold weaknesses of Nineveh (3:12-19)

Overview

The judgement God was proposing to send against Nineveh would be like 'an overflowing flood' that would make 'an utter end' of her. It would be like darkness completely enveloping her (1:8), and would have the following results: (1)Nineveh's name would not be perpetuated (1:14); (2) Her places of worship would be completely destroyed (1:14); (3) She would be completely shamed and humiliated in the eyes of other nations (3:5-6); (4) No one would mourn for her or offer comfort to her (3:7).

God's judgement against Nineveh was certain and inescapable. Conspiring would not prevent it (1:9). Even though everything seemed to be peaceful and prosperous at the time, judgement would come (1:12).

The judgement that would bring devastation to Nineveh would also bring deliverance for the people of Judah. Because Judah failed to repent of her own sins, judgement lay ahead of her at the hands of Babylon, but the fall of Assyria meant no more affliction from her hands and gave Judah the opportunity for peace (1:15). Tragically, Judah failed to seize the opportunity!

Anticipations of Christ

In his opening hymn on the nature of God (1:1-7), Nahum affirms that: (1) God is holy and just; (2) God is long-suffering; (3) God is great in power; (4) God is good and caring. These same characteristics are prominently displayed in God's redeeming work in Christ.

Furthermore, the main teaching of Nahum's prophecy, namely, that God comforts his people by judging their enemies, is a marvellous anticipation of the cross of Christ. There God provided the comfort of salvation for believers by making his Son, Jesus Christ, sin for them and judging their sin in him.

QUESTIONS FOR DISCUSSION

1. Micah names little Bethlehem as the birthplace of the coming Messiah (5:2). Does God delight in using insignificant things to do his work? Read 1 Corinthians 1:26-31. Can you think of examples from the Bible of God using weak, insignificant people?

2. Nahum affirms that God has tremendous wrath against sin (1:2) and yet is good and caring (1:3). Is this a contradiction? How was Jesus' death on the cross at one and the same time a manifestation of God's wrath and his love? Read John 3:16; Romans 3:21-26; 2 Corinthians 5:21.

THE GUIDE

CHAPTER
TWENTY-EIGHT

THE BOOKS OF HABAKKUK AND ZEPHANIAH

BIBLE BOOK

THE BOOKS OF HABAKKUK AND ZEPHANIAH

HABAKKUK

Introduction

Habakkuk, whose name means 'one who embraces' or 'one who clings', prophesied to the nation of Judah shortly before she was taken captive by the Babylonians (Chaldeans) in 586 B.C. Many think Habakkuk prophesied around 600 B.C. during the reign of the evil Jehoiakim.

Purpose and theme

The book of Habakkuk is unique in prophetic literature. The other books are primarily concerned with what the prophets said to their people and contain little of what transpired between the prophet and God. Habakkuk, on the other hand, contains nothing of what he said to the people but consists of what he and God said to each other (1:1 - 2:20) and the prophet's response to this dialogue (3:1-19).

Structure

1. The prophet wrestles with God (1:1 - 2:20)
   a. His first question and God's response (1:1-11)
   b. His second question and God's response (1:12 - 2:20)
2. The prophet rests in God (3:1-19)

Overview

Habakkuk's first question had to do with God's silence. He was living in a society that had the death rattle in its throat, one that was deteriorating and decaying before his eyes. He quickly identifies the major features of his dying nation: violence (1:2), iniquity (1:3), wickedness, strife and contention (1:3), lawlessness (1:4) and injustice (1:4).

In the midst of these things Habakkuk wondered why God was not doing something to set things right. God responded to Habakkuk's question by promising to 'work a work' (1:5), which the prophet would not have believed had someone other than God told him. This work would consist of God using the Chaldeans as his instrument of judgement upon Judah.

God's surprising answer to his first question naturally led Habakkuk to raise a second question: How could a holy God use as his instrument of judgement a nation that was even more sinful than Judah?

God responded to this question by telling Habakkuk to write down certain truths so clearly that anyone reading them could easily understand them and run in obedience to them:

1. God's people should suspend judgement until all the evidence is in. They must not judge him on the basis of what they see here and now. His promises will finally be fulfilled (2:3), and his glory will eventually cover the earth (2:14).

2. The wicked will eventually be judged (2:4-5).

3. The responsibility of the child of God is to live in faith. We are not to vex ourselves with things that are too great for us but rather concern ourselves with those things that God has made clear (2:4). The eye of faith enables us to see that God is even now on his throne (2:20), and evil cannot thwart or defeat him.

The prophecy ends with a great prayer of faith. Habakkuk still did not understand all of God's ways, but he had learned a lesson we all must learn if we are to have peace and tranquillity in this troubled world, that is, to draw our joy from God and what he has done for us in salvation rather than trying to draw it from our circumstances.

TEACHING

Anticipations of Christ

The phrase 'You went forth for the salvation of your people' (3:13) is a marvellous summary of Christ coming to this earth to perform his saving work (Matt. 1:21).

ZEPHANIAH

Introduction

The prophet Zephaniah, whose name means 'Jehovah hides' or 'Jehovah has hidden', may have been born during the terribly dark days of Manasseh's reign in Judah. His name may indicate that his parents, like Moses' parents centuries before, hid him from the atrocities that characterized Manasseh's regime.

Zephaniah himself tells us that he ministered during the days of the good king, Josiah (1:1). Josiah began reigning at the age of eight in 640 B.C. and continued until his death in 609. Zephaniah also prophesied the fall of Nineveh (2:13), an event which occurred in 612 B.C. His ministry must be placed then between 640 and 612 B.C.

Purpose and theme

While Josiah led the nation of Judah into some much needed reforms, the people themselves did not turn to

God with all their hearts. Zephaniah's message was, then, one of judgement to come.

Structure

Zephaniah presented his message in terms of two coming days.

1. The day of retribution (1:1 - 3:8)
2. The day of restoration (3:9-20)

Overview

The nation of Judah was a revolting mess at the time of Zephaniah. Idolatry abounded with pagan priests peacefully co-existing with those who were supposed to be priests of the Lord (1:4). Meanwhile, the worshippers fell into four categories: those who openly worshipped Baal (1:4); those who divided their allegiance between God and Milcom (1:5); those who were apostates, that is, those who had followed the Lord for a while and then turned back (1:6); and those who were indifferent (1:6).

In addition to this religious confusion, there was widespread moral degeneracy. Zephaniah describes the people as 'filthy', 'polluted' and 'oppressing' (3:1). He then offers four specific indictments against them. They refused to:

(1) obey God; (2) receive correction; (3) trust God; (4) draw near to God (3:2).

After describing the people, Zephaniah turns to the leaders: (1) Political leaders used their positions for personal gain and for oppressing the people (3:3); (2) The prophets were 'light' and 'treacherous'. They gave no thought to the truth but simply spoke their own opinions, and this made them dangerous (3:4); (3) The priests showed no reverence for the worship of God or for his law (3:4).

Because of the religious and moral chaos, God was proposing to send shattering judgement. The only way it could be prevented was for leaders and people to gather together around the common goal of repentance (2:1-3). This would encourage God to hide them in the time of judgement (2:3) even as Zephaniah himself had been hidden during Manasseh's reign.

Zephaniah closes his prophecy by looking towards a day of restoration. The forthcoming judgement would cleanse the people of filthy language (3:9); would restore true worship (3:9-10); would cause them to be abundantly ashamed of their doings (3:11); would remove the proud (3:11); and would leave a remnant of faithful people (3:12).

Anticipations of Christ

Several phrases in Zephaniah compel us to think about the work of Christ. 'The LORD has taken away your judgements, he has cast out your enemy' (3:15) may be

applied to our Lord's death, which was designed to deliver us from judgement and to defeat Satan, the great enemy of our souls. 'The King of Israel, the LORD is in your midst...' (3:15,17) reminds us that Jesus was Immanuel, God with us (Matt. 1:23). And the phrase 'The Mighty One, will save...' (3:17) reminds us that Jesus came to save his people from their sins (Matt. 1:21).

QUESTIONS FOR DISCUSSION

1. *Habakkuk deals with the familiar problem of how a good God can allow evil. Where did evil begin? Read Isaiah 14:12-17; John 8:44; 1 John 3:8. How did evil begin in human history? Read Genesis 3:1-7. What has God already done about evil? Read Colossians 2:13-15. What will God do about evil in the future? Read 2 Timothy 4:18.*

2. *Zephaniah charged his people with being 'settled in complacency' (1:12). Read Revelation 3:14-22. Was the church of Laodicea complacent? Why? What did the Lord Jesus challenge her to do? What did he promise to do if she refused?*

CHAPTER
TWENTY-NINE

THE BOOKS OF
HAGGAI
AND ZECHARIAH

BIBLE BOOK

THE BOOKS OF HAGGAI AND ZECHARIAH

HAGGAI

Introduction

The book of Haggai brings us to the post-exilic prophets, that is, those prophets who ministered to the Jews that returned from captivity in Babylon. Haggai, whose name means 'festive', gives us a prophecy that is second only to Obadiah in terms of brevity.

Purpose and theme

The edict of Cyrus in 538 B.C. released the Jews. They returned to their land and immediately began to rebuild the temple, but they soon became so involved in their personal affairs that they stopped working on the temple altogether. For a period of sixteen years, the work stood still. In 520 B.C. Haggai came on the scene to urge the completion of the temple. His ministry was very effective. The people went back to work, and the temple was completed in 516 B.C.

Structure

Haggai consists of four challenging sermons, each of which begins with these words: 'the word of the LORD came by Haggai the prophet'.

1. A sermon of rebuke (1:1-15)
2. A sermon of encouragement (2:1-9)
3. A sermon of rebuke and encouragement (2:10-19)
4. A sermon of encouragement (2:20-23)

Overview

The people of Haggai's time excused themselves from working on the temple because the time was not right (1:2). In his first sermon, Haggai set the record straight. He said the people ceased their work because they were more occupied with their personal comfort than with the work of the Lord (1:4).

In his second sermon, he uncovered yet another reason for the people's reluctance to rebuild the temple: their awareness that it could not match Solomon's temple (2:3). Haggai encouraged them by stating that: (1) The same God who had been with Solomon would be with them (2:5); (2) The absence of gold and silver from their temple would not mean anything to the Lord because he possesses all gold and silver (2:8); (3) Their temple would have greater glory than Solomon's because 'the Desire of All Nations', that is, the Messiah himself, would come to it (2:7,9).

In his third sermon, Haggai reminds the people of the costliness of their disobedience on the matter of rebuilding the temple. The Lord had judged their disobedience by causing their crops to fail, and those failed crops had led to defiled offerings (2:10-17). If they would now acknowledge that the failure of their crops was due to their failure to do God's work (2:18), they would open the door to God's blessings (2:19).

The fourth sermon consists of Haggai sharing with the governor of Judah, Zerubbabel ('descendant of Babylon'), the Lord's promise to bless and honour him (2:20-23).

Anticipations of Christ

1. Christ is 'the Desire of All Nations' (2:7), that is, he is the one who is desirable to all nations, or he is the embodiment of all those things every human heart desires.[1]

2. Christ is pictured in the promises to Zerubbabel who was chosen by the Lord as his signet ring. The signet ring was the precious possession of its owner and a sign of his authority. The Lord Jesus Christ was chosen by God the Father to be his prized instrument in redemption's work and to have all authority in heaven and earth (Matt. 28:18).

ZECHARIAH

Introduction

Zechariah, whose name means 'God remembers', was a younger contemporary of Haggai. The son and grandson of godly men (1:1), Zechariah joined Haggai in encouraging the Jews to rebuild the temple. Zechariah underscored the importance of this task by assuring the people that the Messiah would come to this temple.

Purpose and theme

Irving L. Jensen cites the following purposes for Zechariah:

1. to bring about spiritual revival (1:2-3)
2. to inspire the people to complete the temple (1:16; 4:9)
3. to comfort the people in the midst of their trials (2:13)
4. to assure the people of the coming of the Messiah. Zechariah includes more prophecies of the Messiah than any other book except Isaiah.[2]

Structure

1. Analysis of the present — during the building of the temple (1:1 - 8:23)
   a. A reminder of the past (1:1-6)
   b. Eight comforting visions (1:7 - 6:8)

    c. The comfort of the coronation of Joshua (6:9-15)
    d. A question and four sermons (7:1 - 8:23)

2. Announcement of the future — after the building of the temple (9:1 - 14:21)
    a. The first message (9:1 - 11:17)
    b. The second message (12:1 - 14:21)

Overview

Zechariah begins his prophecy by reminding the people that their forefathers had brought the Babylonian captivity upon themselves by refusing to heed God's call to repentance (1:1-6). He then shares eight comforting visions with the people. These visions occupy most of the first division of the book:

1. Four horsemen announce God's return to Jerusalem and subsequent prosperity (1:7-17).
2. Four craftsmen (agents of God's deliverance) overcome four horns — emblems of the nations that had ruled over Jerusalem (1:18-21).
3. A man measures Jerusalem and discovers it is too small to accommodate all who would come there (2:1-13).
4. The high priest Joshua is cleansed for his work (3:1-10).

5. God is seen as a lampstand with two olive trees, Joshua and Zerubbabel, standing beside him (4:1-14).
6. A flying scroll depicts God's judgement of individual sin (5:1-4).
7. The woman in the basket, representing impurity, depicts God's judgement of national sin (5:5-11).
8. Four charioteers patrol the earth to punish evil (6:1-8).

In the last division of his prophecy, Zechariah delivers two messages. The first deals with the coming of the Messiah and his rejection (9:1 - 11:17). The second message (12:1 - 14:21) presents the future in terms of a day (the phrase 'in that day' appears sixteen times in the last three chapters). This day is the entire gospel age that was to begin with the coming of Christ and close at the end of time. It is an age of hostility towards the people of God and God's protective care of his own (12:1-5), an age of the open fountain, that is, of cleansing from sin through the finished work of Christ (13:1-2), and an age that will culminate in light and life (14:6-9).

Anticipations of Christ

Prophecy	Fulfilment
Servant (3:8)	Mark 10:45
Branch (93:8; 6:12)	Luke 1:78
King-Priest (6:13)	Hebrews 6:20 - 7:1
Lowly King (9:9-10)	Matthew 21:4-5; John 12:14-16

Betrayed (11:12-13)	Matthew 27:9
Hands pierced (12:10)	John 19:37
Cleansing fountain (13:1)	Revelation 1:5
Humanity and deity (13:7; 6:12)	John 8:40; 1:1
Smitten shepherd (13:7-9)	Matthew 26:31; Mark 14:27
Second Coming and coronation (14:5,9)	John 10:16; Revelation 11:15; 21:27[3]

DISCUSS IT

QUESTIONS FOR DISCUSSION

1. The people of Haggai's day were guilty of mistaken priorities in that they were putting their own comfort above the work of the Lord. What are some of the priorities of the child of God? Read Matthew 6:33; 22:34-40; Colossians 3:1-25; 1 Peter 2:9-10.

2. Zechariah ministered to those who had returned from exile in Babylon. He reminded them that the exile had been promised by God, that even though their fathers had run from the Word of God, it had finally overtaken them. What are some other examples of God's word of judgement catching up with people? Read 1 Samuel 13:1-15; 15:10-29; 31:1-10; 1 Kings 13:1 - 14:18; 15:27-30; Daniel 5:1-31.

CHAPTER THIRTY

THE BOOK OF MALACHI AND THE INTER-TESTAMENTAL PERIOD

MALACHI

THE BOOK OF MALACHI AND THE INTER-TESTAMENTAL PERIOD

Introduction

INTRODUCTION

Malachi ('my messenger') was another of the prophets who ministered to the people of Israel after they returned from their captivity in Babylon. When Malachi came on the scene the temple had already been rebuilt and the sacrifices had resumed. Many think Malachi conducted his ministry between the years of 432 and 425 B.C., that is, during the period of time that Nehemiah was back in Babylon (see Post-Exilic Timeline, pp. 11-12).

Purpose

All was not well in Malachi's time. Miles Bennett describes the situation in this way: 'A spirit of dull depression had settled over the inhabitants of Jerusalem; scepticism and spiritual indifference held the people in their grasp... The flood of skepticism abroad in the land affected both the people and their religious leaders. Religion became largely a matter of ritual. Apathy and stinginess toward God prevailed.'[1]

How did the people get into such a state? Joyce Baldwin answers: '...the Temple had been completed, but nothing momentous had occurred to indicate that God's presence had returned to fill it with glory'. In other words, nothing had happened to indicate that the glorious prophecies of Haggai and Zechariah were going to be fulfilled. Consequently, in the words of Baldwin, 'The round of religious duties continued to be carried on, but without enthusiasm.'[2]

God's answer to the condition of the people was to send Malachi to carry on a dialogue with the people. There are seven occurrences of dialogue in which God makes an accusation, the people raise an objection and God refutes the objection (1:2-5; 1:6 - 2:9; 2:10-16; 2:17 - 3:6; 3:7-12; 3:13-15).

Structure

The prophecy of Malachi can be divided as follows:

1. The blessing of the nation (1:1-5)

2. The sinfulness of the nation (1:6 - 3:16)
   a. The sinfulness of the priests (1:6 - 2:9)
      • Dishonouring God's name (1:6-9)
      • Despising God's service (1:10 - 2:7)
      • Breaking God's laws (2:8-9)

b. The sinfulness of the people (2:10 - 3:16)
- Breaking commitments (2:10-16)
- Expressing unbelief (2:17 - 3:6)
- Robbing God (3:7-12)
- Speaking against God (3:13-16)

3. The consolation of the nation (3:17 - 4:6)
   a. The coming of the Messiah (3:1-6)
   b. The present demand (3:7-12)

Overview

The book of Malachi is a very shocking book. We are surprised to find the Jewish nation in such a terrible state after the Babylonian captivity. By the time Malachi came on the scene, the captivity had been over for more than one hundred years. Although that is a substantial period of time, it was such a traumatic event that we would have thought that its lessons would not have been forgotten. But the people of Malachi's generation were showing signs of doing that very thing. The nation began to disregard her special covenant relationship with God (1:1-5) as both priests (1:6 - 2:9) and people plunged into sinful behaviour (2:10 - 3:15).

While they kept up the various religious observances the priests and people quite obviously did not have their hearts in what they were doing.

The priests brought defiled sacrifices to God and complained about how tiresome the religious duties were (1:7-8,13). Meanwhile the people thought nothing at all about disregarding God's laws regarding marriage (2:14-16) or about withholding their tithes (3:8-10). They also regarded service to God as vain and meaningless (3:13-15). Furthermore, the people seem to have all but lost faith in the coming of their Messiah (3:1).

Using the question and answer method, Malachi confronts the priests and the people with their sins. He affirms that the promised Messiah was indeed coming, but he warned that this coming would not be a happy event for sinful people (3:1-6; 4:1-6).

Anticipations of Christ

The following are announced by Malachi:

1. The ministry of the forerunner of the Messiah, John the Baptist (3:1; 4:5-6; see Luke 1:76; Matt. 11:14).

2. The coming of Christ to his temple (3:2-3; see Matt. 21:12-13; Mark 11:15-17; Luke 19:45-46; John 2:13-22).

3. The Messiah as 'The Sun of Righteousness' who rises with 'healing in his wings' (4:2).

THE INTER-TESTAMENTAL PERIOD

The four hundred years between the end of the Old Testament era and the beginning of the New Testament era were extremely significant. During those years the Israel to which Jesus came was formed.

Political developments

The Persian Empire, which conquered Babylon and released the Jews from their captivity, continued to control Israel for approximately 200 years from the time of their restoration to their homeland.

Between 334 and 331 B.C., Alexander the Great defeated the Persian king, Darius III, in three decisive battles. With the defeat of Persia, Israel came under the control of the Greeks. After Alexander's death in 323 B.C., his empire was divided into four parts, and Israel came under the control of the Ptolemies of Egypt. In 198 B.C., Antiochus III of the Seleucid Empire, named after the descendants of one of Alexander's generals, Seleucus, defeated the Ptolemies and took control of Israel. The *MacArthur Study Bible* says of this time: 'Antiochus desecrated and plundered the temple of Jerusalem in 170 B.C. In 167 B.C., Antiochus ordered Hellenization in Palestine and forbade the Jews from keeping their laws, observing the Sabbath, keeping festivals, offering sacrifices, and circumcising their children. Copies of the Torah were ordered destroyed, idolatrous altars were set up, plus the Jews were commanded by Antiochus to offer unclean sacrifices and to eat swine's flesh.'

The rule of Antiochus continued until Mattathias and his five sons led the Maccabean Revolt. After twenty-four years of war (166-142 B.C.), Israel became independent, and the Hasmonean dynasty was established. The name 'Hasmonean' was derived from 'Hashmon', an ancestor of the Maccabees. The Hasmonean dynasty ended in 63 B.C. when the Roman general, Pompey, conquered the land of Israel.

Religious developments

Septuagint — The Greek influence during the intertestamental period led to this Greek translation of the Old Testament. The word 'Septuagint', the Latin word for seventy, was derived from the seventy scholars who produced this translation. The Septuagint is often designated by LXX (the Roman numerals for seventy).

Pharisees ('separated ones') — This largest and most influential of the religious parties in Judaism began during the era of the Maccabees. The Pharisees developed and emphasized an oral tradition in addition to the written law of Moses, and they sought to make this tradition binding on all Jews.

Sadducees — The aristocratic, wealthy Sadducees claimed to be descendants of Zadok, the high priest during Solomon's reign. They opposed the Pharisees' emphasis on oral law and stressed the first five books of the Old Testament as the ultimate authority. They did not believe in life after death or in the existence of angels or demons. Politically oriented, they tended to support the government no matter who was running it.

⟨QUESTIONS FOR DISCUSSION⟩

1. *Malachi sternly rebuked the religious leaders of his day for not being true messengers of the Lord (2:1-9). What is the message of a true minister of God? Read Romans 1:16-17; 1 Corinthians 1:17-25; 2:1-5; 4:1-2; 2 Corinthians 5:12-21; 2 Timothy 4:1-5.*

2. *As the people of Malachi's day awaited the first coming of Christ, so Christians today await his Second Coming. How are we to wait? Read 2 Peter 3:1-18.*

3. *Jesus had several encounters with both the Pharisees and the Sadducees. How did he explain the legalism of the former and the resurrection scepticism of the latter? Read Mark 7:1-13; 12:18-27.*

THE GUIDE

CHAPTER
THIRTY-ONE

THE GOSPEL OF MATTHEW

BIBLE BOOK

THE GOSPEL OF MATTHEW

Introduction

The first of the four Gospels was written by Matthew ('gift of the Lord'). When the Lord Jesus Christ found him, Matthew was a despised publican, that is, a Jew who collected taxes for the Roman government. Jesus simply said to him, 'Follow me!', and Matthew immediately 'arose and followed him' (Matt. 9:9), becoming one of Jesus' twelve disciples.

Matthew's authorship of this Gospel has been widely accepted through the centuries. Although he is nowhere named as the author, some early manuscripts do have the words 'according to Matthew' in the title. The date of the Gospel is usually put between A.D. 50 and 70.

Purpose and theme

Matthew wrote to a predominantly Jewish readership. His great purpose in doing so was to demonstrate that Jesus of Nazareth was the fulfilment of the Old Testament prophecies, and was, therefore, the Messiah of whom the Old Testament spoke. The phrase 'that it might be fulfilled' occurs twelve times in this Gospel.

Other indications that Matthew wrote to a Jewish readership are as follows:

1. The opening genealogy that traces Jesus back to Abraham, the father of the Jewish nation
2. The frequent references to Jesus as 'the Son of David' (1:1; 9:27; 12:23; 15:22; 20:30)
3. The numerous quotations from the Old Testament
4. The phrase 'the King of the Jews', which occurs four times (2:2; 27:11,29,37)

Additional distinctive features

1. The word 'kingdom' appears fifty-five times and the phrase 'the kingdom of heaven' thirty-two times.
2. The Gospel includes five major discourses (5:1 - 7:29; 10:1-42;13:1-52; 18:1-35; 24:1 - 25:46).
3. The Sadducees are mentioned here more than in any other Gospel.

Relationship to the other Gospels

Some people have been troubled by the fact that there are four Gospels. There would perhaps have been less confusion if there had been one very detailed account of the life of Christ. Why then do we have four? The answer is that each Gospel was written for a different group and from a unique perspective. The Gospels do not contradict but rather complement each other. In addition to Matthew's distinctive emphasis on Jesus as king, we have the following:

- Mark — Jesus as servant
- Luke — Jesus as the Son of Man
- John — Jesus as the Son of God

This is not to say that the theme of one Gospel is not found in the others. It is rather a matter of emphasis.

The first three Gospels are called 'synoptic' Gospels, that is, 'affording a general, same or collective view'. While not contradicting the synoptics, in the Gospel of John there is much more information about Jesus.

Structure

Matthew's Gospel lends itself to the following structure:

1. Introduction (1:1 - 4:11)
2. Jesus' ministry in Galilee (4:12 - 18:35)
3. Jesus' ministry in Judea (19:1 - 25:46)
4. Jesus' death and resurrection (26:1 - 28:20)

Overview

Introduction (1:1 - 4:11)

Matthew begins his Gospel with a genealogy (1:1-17) in which he shows that Jesus, the Messiah, was indeed the Son of David and the Son of Abraham (1:1), just as God had promised.

He proceeds to show how the birth of Jesus fulfilled prophecy.

Prophecy	*Fulfilment*
Isaiah 7:14	Matthew 1:22-23
Isaiah 11:1	Matthew 2:23
Jeremiah 31:15	Matthew 2:17-18
Hosea 11:1	Matthew 2:15
Micah 5:2	Matthew 2:5-6

After presenting the ministry of John the Baptist, the forerunner of Christ, as the fulfilment of prophecy (Isa. 40:3; Matt. 3:3), Matthew relates both the baptism and temptations of Jesus (Matt. 3:13 - 4:11).

Jesus' ministry in Galilee (4:12 - 18:35)

This section of the Gospel consists of the Sermon on the Mount (5:1 - 7:29), the mighty works of Christ (8:1 - 11:1), the increasing rejection of him (11:2 - 16:12), and his preparation of his disciples for what lay ahead (16:13 - 18:35).

In the Sermon on the Mount (5:1 - 7:29), Jesus deals with his kingdom as a different kind of kingdom. In the discourse, he rejects both Pharisaic interpretation of the Law of Moses (5:3-16) and Pharisaic practices (5:17 - 7:29).

After relating the sermon, Matthew turns his attention to the works of Jesus in Galilee. In chapters 8-10, he presents ten miracles performed by the Lord (8:1-4,5-13,14-15,23-27,28-34; 9:1-8,18-22,23-26,27-31,32-34). In chapters 11-18, he proceeds to show the increasing rejection of Christ and Jesus' preparation of his disciples for what was lying ahead. This section contains Jesus' kingdom parables (ch. 13), his promise to build his church (16:18) and his transfiguration (17:1-13).

Jesus' ministry in Judea (19:1 - 25:46)

Matthew brings us to the major turning point in his Gospel with these words: 'Now it came to pass, when Jesus had finished these sayings, that he departed from Galilee and came to the region of Judea beyond the Jordan' (19:1).

After arriving in Judea, Jesus rode into Jerusalem in triumph (Matt. 21:1-11). He was hailed on this day because those present in Jerusalem for the Passover believed he would finally declare himself to be king and would proceed to lead Israel to victory over her enemies.

His triumphal entry into the city began the last week of his public ministry, a week that was marked by controversy with the religious leaders (21:23 - 23:39) and by Jesus instructing his disciples about the future (24:1 - 25:46).

Jesus' death and resurrection (26:1 - 28:20)

The Jews' rejection of Jesus culminated in his arrest, trial and crucifixion. The fact that his public ministry ended in this way would seem to be proof positive that he could not possibly be the Messiah, but, as Matthew indicates, his death was itself a fulfilment of prophecy (27:35). Furthermore, the fact that the veil of the temple was torn from top to bottom at the exact moment of his death was a striking sign that it constituted the perfect sacrifice for sinners and there was no further need for the anticipatory animal sacrifices of the Old Testament era (27:51).

The greatest proof of Jesus' messiahship was, of course, his resurrection from the grave on the third day, an event that was amply proven by those who saw the empty tomb and the many who encountered the risen Christ.

QUESTIONS FOR DISCUSSION

1. *Matthew presents Christ as king. Some of the Old Testament prophecies about the kingship of Christ are*

DISCUSS IT

found in Genesis 49:10; Numbers 24:17; Psalm 2:1-12; Isaiah 9:6-7; Jeremiah 23:5-8; and Daniel 7:9-14. What do we learn about the kingship of Christ from these passages?

2. What vital role do the miracles of Jesus play in the Gospels? Read Mark 16:19-20; John 20:30-31; Hebrews 2:1-4.

3. John's Gospel records six confessions of faith that are similar to the centurion's in Matthew 27:54. Read John 1:34,49; 6:69; 11:27; 20:28,31. Who offered these confessions?

CHAPTER
THIRTY-TWO

THE GOSPEL OF MARK

BIBLE BOOK

THE GOSPEL OF MARK

Introduction

Almost all agree that John Mark was the author of this Gospel — the John Mark who lived in Jerusalem with his mother Mary (Acts 12:12), who, according to conjecture, fled from the garden when Jesus was arrested (Mark 14:51-52), and who caused a split between Barnabas (Col. 4:10) and Paul by forsaking them on their first missionary journey (Acts 13:13). Mark had a very close relationship with Simon Peter (who calls him 'my son' in 1 Peter 5:13), and most think his Gospel is based on information from the apostle.

Bible scholars are divided on the question of when Mark wrote his Gospel. Answers range from A.D. 40 to 75.

Purpose

Each of the four Gospels has its own distinct emphasis. Matthew presents Jesus as king, Luke as the Son of Man, and John as the Son of God. Mark's emphasis is clearly set out in these words:

'For even the Son of Man did not come to be served, but to serve, and to give his life a ransom for many' (10:45).

Mark's purpose, therefore, is to present Christ as servant. Another way of putting it is like this — in Matthew we have royalty, in Luke humanity, in John deity, and in Mark humility.

Distinctive features

Mark's Gospel has certain distinct characteristics:

1. *Compactness* (Luke has 1147 verses, Matthew 1068, and Mark 661).

2. *Action*. Mark dwells on the works of Jesus instead of on his words.

There are only four parables in Mark (Matthew has nineteen, Luke has twenty-seven). Mark records only one of Jesus' discourses (13:1-37). Matthew has six. Sixty per cent of Matthew and fifty-one per cent of Luke consist of the words of Jesus, while only forty-two per cent of Mark is devoted to the same.

Mark's favourite word also conveys action. He uses the word 'immediately' (sometimes translated 'straightway') a total of forty-two times. There are only seven occurrences of this word in Matthew and one in Luke.

The conjunction 'and' also appears frequently (it begins twelve of the sixteen chapters), and adds to the

impression of action and crispness. Mark also frequently uses what is called the historical present tense — Jesus comes, Jesus says, Jesus heals (a total of 150 times).

Structure

1. Introduction (1:1-13)
2. The service in Galilee (1:14 - 9:50)
3. The sacrifice in Jerusalem (10:1 - 15:47)
4. Conclusion (16:1-20)

Overview

Introduction (1:1-13)

Mark crams into his introduction very brief accounts of the ministry of John the Baptist (1:1-8), the baptism of Jesus (1:9-11) and the temptations of Jesus (1:12-13). Before he began his public ministry Jesus was announced by the forerunner (as prophesied in the Old Testament), identified with sinners, approved by the Father and victorious over the enemy.

The service in Galilee (1:14 - 9:50)

Mark launches his account of Jesus' public ministry by affirming that he, Jesus, came into

Galilee preaching, 'The time is fulfilled, and the king-dom of God is at hand. Repent, and believe in the gospel' (1:14-15).

The phrase 'the time is fulfilled' means the time ap-pointed by God to fulfil his promises of redemption had come. 'The kingdom of God is at hand' reveals that the kingdom had, in the person of Jesus, come right into the midst of the lives of his hearers. 'Repent, and believe' shows that the people had to change their minds about sin, make a radical break with it and submit completely to God's rule in their lives.

After introducing Jesus' ministry, Mark proceeds in whirlwind fashion to relate many of the works Jesus performed in Galilee, a large number of which referred to the casting out of demons (1:21-28; 3:11-12) and the sick being healed (1:29 - 2:12; 3:10; 5:25-34; 6:53-56; 7:24-30,31-37).

There were also instances of Jesus' authority over nature (4:35-41; 6:32-44,45-52; 8:1-10), and even an episode of Jesus raising the dead (5:35-43).

Jesus' ministry in Galilee was further marked by con-troversy with the religious leaders over his claim to forgive sins (2:6-12) and his sabbath practices (3:1-5).

The sacrifice in Jerusalem (10:1 - 15:47)

The major turning point in the Gospel comes with these words: 'Then he arose from there and came to the re-gion of Judea by the other side of the Jordan' (10:1).

Jesus had already predicted his death (8:31-33; 9:30-31), and now he begins the journey he knew would

TEACHING

culminate in his crucifixion. In the course of his journey to Jerusalem, he continues his teaching ministry (10:1-16,23-45), deals with the rich young ruler (10:17-22) and heals blind Bartimaeus (10:46-52). The teaching of Jesus in this section brings us to the Gospel's most powerful emphasis on servanthood. Jesus seized the request of James and John for positions of prominence in his kingdom to drive home this vital lesson: greatness in his kingdom is achieved through humble service. He said: 'Whoever of you desires to be first shall be slave of all. For even the Son of Man did not come to be served, but to serve, and to give his life a ransom for many' (10:44-45).

With his journey complete, he triumphantly enters Jerusalem and embarks upon his final week of ministry, a week that was marked by teaching his disciples and controversy with the religious leaders. He then went to the cross of Calvary and offered his life as that 'ransom for many'.

Conclusion (16:1-20)

Death could not hold the Lord Jesus Christ. On the third day, he arose from the grave, giving indisputable proof that he was indeed the Son of God and that his redemptive work was approved of God and fully sufficient.

QUESTIONS FOR DISCUSSION

1. *Mark stresses the humility of Christ. For more about this, read John 13:1-20. Why did Jesus wash his disciples' feet? What can we do to 'wash the feet' of others?*

2. *What are some essential ingredients in serving God? Read Psalm 2:11; 101:6; Matthew 6:24; Romans 7:6; 12:1-21.*

THE GUIDE

CHAPTER
THIRTY-THREE

THE GOSPEL OF
LUKE

LUKE

THE GOSPEL OF LUKE

Introduction

INTRODUCTION

The Gospel of Luke was written by Luke, the beloved physician who accompanied Paul on his missionary travels. While not an eyewitness of the events he recorded, Luke carefully researched them (1:1-4). His Gospel is addressed to 'Theophilus', 'lover of God' or 'loved by God' (1:3). Some take this name as a literary device, that is, they see it as Luke's way of addressing all who loved God. Most evangelical commentators regard Theophilus as a historical figure.

The date of Luke's Gospel is usually set around A.D. 60, before Jerusalem's destruction in A.D. 70.

Purpose

The Gospel of Luke stresses the humanity of Jesus.

1. The prominent title for Jesus is 'Son of Man'.
2. Luke goes into greater detail than the other

Gospels about the birth of Jesus and also includes a section on the boyhood of Jesus, which is not mentioned at all in the other Gospels.

3. Luke stresses Jesus' dependence on prayer.
4. Luke stresses Jesus' human poverty.
5. Luke stresses Jesus' human sympathies.

Luke focuses on the humanity of Jesus as an essential part of Jesus' saving work. It was 'to seek and to save that which was lost' (19:10) that the second person of the Trinity took unto himself our humanity.

Distinctive features

1. All four Gospels relate something of the ministry of John the Baptist, but Luke includes the greatest details. He alone relates the birth of the great forerunner (1:5-25,57-80).

2. Luke gives special prominence to women. He alone mentions the mother of John the Baptist, Elizabeth (1:5-7,39-45,57-58), and the adoration of the prophetess Anna (2:36-38). Women are also emphasized in the following passages: 7:37-50; 10:38-42; 15:8-10; 23:27-31.

3. Many commentators think Luke was a Gentile. If this is so, he is the only Gentile contributor to Scripture.

Structure

1. Introduction (1:1-4)
2. The birth and childhood of Jesus (1:5 - 2:52)
3. The prelude to ministry (3:1 - 4:13)
4. The ministry in Galilee (4:14 - 9:50)
5. The journey to Jerusalem (9:51 - 19:27)
6. The last week of Jesus (19:28 - 23:56)
7. The resurrection and its aftermath (24:1-53)

Overview

Introduction (1:1-4)

Luke begins his Gospel by declaring his intention to write an orderly narrative of those things 'most surely believed' among Christians. The church is a community of faith, a community that tenaciously holds with overpowering conviction to a distinct body of truths.

The birth and childhood of Jesus (1:5 - 2:52)

After introducing his Gospel, Luke recounts visits of the angel Gabriel to Zacharias to announce the birth of John the Baptist (1:5-25) and to Mary to announce the birth of Jesus (1:26-33). Both announcements came true to the last detail. The birth of Jesus occurred in Bethlehem, fulfilling the Old Testament prophecy of Micah (Micah 5:2).

The prelude to ministry (3:1 - 4:13)

The public ministry of Jesus was preceded by the ministry of John the Baptist (3:1-20), the baptism of Jesus by John (3:21-22) and the temptations of Jesus in the wilderness (4:1-13). It should also be noted that Luke, like Matthew, includes a genealogy of Jesus. Matthew's genealogy begins with Abraham and traces the lineage to Joseph. Luke begins with Jesus and traces his lineage all the way back to God himself. Matthew's genealogy is the legal lineage of Jesus through Joseph. Luke's is the personal lineage of Jesus through his mother Mary.

The ministry in Galilee (4:14 - 9:50)

Luke includes a great variety of details in this part of his Gospel. Accounts of demons being cast out (4:31-37; 8:26-39; 9:37-42) and the sick being healed (4:38-39; 5:12-15,17-26; 6:6-11; 7:1-10; 8:41-48) are intertwined with various parables (5:36-39; 7:40-50; 8:4-18), the Sermon on the Mount (6:20-49), controversies with religious leaders (6:1-11), and a host of other details. This portion of the Gospel also includes two accounts of Jesus raising the dead (7:11-16; 8:49-56).

The journey to Jerusalem (9:51 - 19:27)

One of the most fascinating parts of Luke's Gospel is the way in which he sets the final journey of Jesus to Jerusalem in such bold relief. Luke records the

beginning of this journey with these words: 'Now it came to pass, when the time had come for him to be received up, that he steadfastly set his face to go to Jerusalem...' (9:51).

It should not escape our attention that the major part of this Gospel is devoted to this final journey to Jerusalem and Jesus' death there. This underscores for us the importance of Jesus' redeeming death.

In this section, Luke also shifts the focus from the acts of Jesus to his teachings.

The last week of Jesus (19:28 - 23:56)

Luke's description of Jesus' last week covers much the same ground as Matthew and Mark. He includes an account of the triumphal entry (19:28-39), but adds the interesting detail of Jesus weeping as he approached the city of Jerusalem (19:41-44). The cleansing of the temple (19:45-48), controversies with the religious leaders (20:1-47), and instructions to the disciples (21:1-38) are also included in this section. Luke devotes considerable attention to the night before the crucifixion. He covers Jesus' last supper with his disciples (22:1-38), his prayer in Gethsemane (22:39-46), the betrayal of Judas Iscariot (22:47-53), the denials of Simon Peter (22:54-62), and the trials of Jesus (22:66 - 23:25).

All this culminated in Jesus being crucified (23:26-49) and buried (23:50-56). In his account of the crucifixion Luke includes three of the seven words Jesus spoke from the cross, words not related by the other Gospels:

1. 'Father, forgive them, for they do not know what they do' (23:34).
2. 'Assuredly, I say to you, today you will be with me in Paradise' (23:43).
3. 'Father, into your hands I commit my spirit' (23:46).

The resurrection and its aftermath (24:1-53)

While Luke shares details of the resurrection found in Matthew and Mark, he significantly adds to our knowledge of it by including the story of the risen Christ journeying along the road to Emmaus with two of his disciples. It was during this journey, and while these men had not yet recognized Jesus, that he gave his people of all ages the key for interpreting the Scriptures in that he 'expounded to them in all the Scriptures the things concerning himself' (24:27).

When Jesus later appeared in Jerusalem to eleven of his original twelve disciples, he explained his crucifixion and resurrection in this way: 'These are the words which I spoke to you while I was still with you, that all things must be fulfilled which were written in the Law of Moses and the Prophets and the Psalms concerning me' (24:44).

The Lord Jesus Christ is, therefore, the great subject and focus of Scripture, and we only handle Scripture correctly if we look for him.

DISCUSS IT

QUESTIONS FOR DISCUSSION

1. The life of Jesus calls us to pray. What kinds of prayer are we to offer? Read Matthew 6:6; 1 Timothy 2:1-3; Hebrews 4:14-16; James 5:13-18; 1 John 1:9; 5:14-15.

2. Only Luke reports this statement Jesus made from the cross: '...today you will be with me in paradise' (23:43). What does the word 'paradise' mean? Read 2 Corinthians 12:4; Revelation 2:7.

CHAPTER
THIRTY-FOUR

THE GOSPEL OF JOHN

THE GOSPEL OF JOHN

Introduction

JOHN

INTRODUCTION

The Gospel of John is perhaps the best loved of all the books of the Bible. The early Christians used the eagle to symbolize this Gospel, and most of us readily agree it is a fitting symbol indeed because the Gospel causes our minds and hearts to soar.

It was written by John, one of the sons of Zebedee and one of the three disciples in Jesus' inner circle. It is usually dated at A.D. 90, and it is traditionally believed to have been addressed to Christians in Ephesus, located on the west coast of Asia Minor.

Purpose

John did not leave his readers to speculate about his purpose. Towards the end of the Gospel, he lays it out in these words: ' ...these are written that you may believe that Jesus is the Christ, the Son of God, and that believing you may have life in his name' (20:31).

John wrote his Gospel, then, to emphasize the deity of the Lord Jesus Christ and to encourage his readers to believe in Christ. While John was most certainly interested in convincing unbelievers who might read his Gospel, he was actually writing to fellow-Christians. The force of the word 'believe' in the above verse is 'that you may go on believing'.

If the above date is accurate, it had been almost sixty years since Jesus had ascended to the Father in heaven. Many false teachers had arisen to challenge the basic facts of the gospel. John wrote to encourage his readers not to be swayed by these teachers. We might imagine him taking up his pen as he said to himself: 'If these young Christians could see what I saw and hear what I heard, they would not be influenced by falsehood.'

Distinctive features

1. Seven 'I am' sayings are found in John
   'I am the bread of life' (6:35)
   'I am the light of the world' (8:12)
   'I am the door' (10:7)
   'I am the good shepherd' (10:11)
   'I am the resurrection and the life' (11:25)
   'I am the way, the truth, and the life' (14:6)
   'I am the true vine' (15:1)

2. John also includes seven signs performed by Jesus
   changing water into wine (2:1-11)
   healing the nobleman's son (4:46-54)

healing the lame man (5:1-9)
feeding the five thousand (6:1-14)
walking on water (6:15-21)
healing the blind man (9:1-7)
raising Lazarus from the grave (11:38-44)

3. John's Gospel contains a powerful emphasis on a particular hour (2:4; 7:6,8,30; 8:20; 12:23,27-28; 13:1; 17:1).

4. Key words in John's Gospel are: believe (98 times), world (78), Jews (71), know (55), glorify (42), my Father (35).

Structure

1. The prologue (1:1-18)
2. The public ministry of Jesus (1:19 - 12:50)
3. The private ministry of Jesus (13:1 - 17:26)
4. The crucifixion and resurrection of Jesus (18:1 - 20:29)
5. Epilogue (20:30 - 21:25)

Overview

The prologue (1:1-18)

The false teachers, known as 'gnostics', were championing a whole cluster of beliefs that essentially gutted the Christian message. Some denied that Jesus was equal to God before he came into this world and maintained that he was the least in a whole series of gods under the true God. Another common belief was that Jesus was not really God after he was born in Bethlehem. In the prologue John launches a frontal attack on these beliefs by showing that Jesus was God before he came into this world, and he was still God while he was here.

The public ministry of Jesus (1:19 - 12:50)

John's account of the public ministry of Jesus may itself be divided into two major parts. In the first part (1:19 - 4:54) Jesus reveals himself to ever-widening circles and is initially well received: to John the Baptist (1:19-34), to his disciples (1:35 - 2:12), to Jerusalem (2:13 - 3:21), to Judea (3:22-36), to Samaria (4:1-45) and to Galilee (4:46-54). John includes in his account several episodes not related in the other Gospels: the miracle at Cana (2:1-11), the discussions with Nicodemus (3:1-15) and the Samaritan woman (4:1-42), the healing of the nobleman's son (4:46-54).

In the second section (5:1 - 12:50), Jesus performs further signs, enrages the religious establishment and encounters fierce opposition in both Jerusalem (5:1-47; 7:1 - 11:57) and in Galilee (6:1-71). Also in this section John also includes much material not found in the other Gospels. Some of the accounts unique to John are: the healing of the lame man and the subsequent Sabbath controversy (5:1-47), the bread of life discourse

(6:32-66), the healing of the blind man and the subsequent controversy (9:1-41), the Good Shepherd discourse (10:1-42) and the raising of Lazarus (11:1-57).

The private ministry of Jesus (13:1 - 17:26)

John shifts attention to Jesus' private ministry (to his disciples) with these words: 'Now before the feast of the Passover, when Jesus knew that his hour had come that he should depart from this world to the Father, having loved his own who were in the world, he loved them to the end' (13:1).

After this introduction, John proceeds to describe the night before the crucifixion. At that time Jesus washed his disciples' feet (13:2-20) and shared with them some of the most tender and comforting teachings to be found anywhere in Scripture (14:1 - 16:33). It is this portion of the Gospel that contains these greatly loved words from Jesus: 'Let not your heart be troubled; you believe in God, believe also in me. In my Father's house are many mansions; if it were not so, I would have told you. I go to prepare a place for you. And if I go and prepare a place for you, I will come again and receive you to myself; that where I am, there you may be also' (14:1-3).

On that same night, Jesus prayed with his disciples (presumably as they made their way to the Garden of Gethsemane where he was arrested). This beautiful prayer consists of Jesus praying for himself (17:1-5), for his disciples at that time (17:6-19) and for his future disciples (17:20-26).

The crucifixion and resurrection of Jesus (18:1 - 20:29)

John recounts with more detail than any other Gospel writer the series of trials that Jesus endured. He gives special attention to Jesus' encounter with Pilate (18:28 - 19:16). After the trials were over and Jesus was condemned, the Roman soldiers led him to Golgotha where he was crucified. Unique to John are three of the seven words Jesus spoke from the cross:

- 'Woman, behold your son!' (19:26)
- 'I thirst!' (19:28)
- 'It is finished!' (19:30)

After being crucified, Jesus arose from the grave, and John again includes details not shared by the synoptic Gospels.

Epilogue (20:30 - 21:25)

John closes his Gospel, as we have noted, with a statement of his purpose (20:30-31). He then includes an account of the risen Christ following his disciples to the Sea of Tiberias, where he reinstated Simon Peter. His thrice-repeated question: 'Do you love me?' (21:15,16,17) effectively reversed Simon's threefold denial.

QUESTIONS FOR DISCUSSION

DISCUSS IT

1. *The new birth of which Jesus spoke in John 3 is presented in other passages. Read James 1:18; 1 Peter 1:23. What instrument does God use in producing the new birth? Read 1 Peter 2:1-3; 1 John 2:29; 3:9-10; 5:4. What does the new birth produce?*

2. *Read Acts 2. Jesus' promise to send the Holy Spirit upon his disciples was fulfilled on what day? What signs accompanied his coming? What were the results of it?*

CHAPTER
THIRTY-FIVE

THE ACTS OF
THE APOSTLES

ACTS

BIBLE BOOK

THE ACTS OF THE APOSTLES

Introduction

The Acts of the Apostles was written by Luke. The *MacArthur Study Bible* says: 'Luke was Paul's close friend, travelling companion, and personal physician (Col. 4:14). He was a careful researcher (Luke 1:1-4) and an accurate historian, displaying an intimate knowledge of Roman laws and customs, as well as the geography of Palestine, Asia Minor, and Italy.'[1]

While various dates have been suggested for Acts, the most probable seems to be around A.D. 60. The fact that Luke is silent about the great persecution under Nero (A.D. 64) and about the death of Paul (A.D. 68) indicates that he wrote before these events.

Purpose

Acts begins with a tiny group of Jesus' disciples gathered in a room in Jerusalem, the capital of Judaism. It ends with its foremost spokesman and leader, Paul, preaching the gospel without hindrance in Rome, the capital of the civilized world (28:30-31).

Detailing how the gospel progressed from that modest provincial beginning to its impressive ending was Luke's purpose in writing. He recounts the church's struggle to break out of its Jewish mould and to obey the command of Christ by carrying the gospel to the ends of the earth (1:8). Acts is the account of the struggle for an unhindered gospel.

This book makes for exhilarating reading. It is a fast-paced account of conversions, great numbers of conversions, notable conversions and conversions in the metropolitan areas.

It is not uncommon to hear someone refer to the book of Acts as 'The Acts of the Holy Spirit' or even 'The Gospel of the Holy Spirit'. Such references give the impression that when we come to the book of Acts our dealings with Christ are over, that he ceases to be central. Actually the book of Acts continues the story of Christ. It is the account of what the reigning Christ accomplished through his church, which he empowered with his gift of the Holy Spirit.

Distinctive features

1. The Holy Spirit is mentioned about seventy times.
2. The word 'witness' is used thirty times. It first appears in the book's key verse (1:8).

TEACHING

3. The 'we' passages in the latter half of the book show that Luke accompanied Paul in some of his travels.

Structure

1. The gospel breaks out of Judaism — main character, Simon Peter (1:1 - 12:24)
   a. Preparation for the struggle for an unhindered gospel (1:1 - 8:3)
      - the instructions of Jesus (1:1-26)
      - the outpouring of the Spirit (2:1-47)
      - various trials (3:1 - 8:3)
   b. Major turning points in the struggle (8:4 - 12:24)
      - Philip catches the vision (8:4-40)
      - Saul of Tarsus is converted (9:1-43)
      - Simon Peter joins the struggle (10:1 - 11:30)
      - Persecution is renewed by Herod (12:1-24)

2. The gospel goes to the uttermost parts of the earth — main character, Paul (12:25 - 28:31)
   a. The missionary journeys of Paul (12:25 - 20:38)
   b. The trip to Jerusalem (21:1 - 23:35)
   c. Paul before prominent officials (24:1 - 26:32)
   d. Paul journeying to and ministering in Rome (27:1 - 28:31)

Overview

The gospel breaks out of Judaism — main character,
Simon Peter (1:1 - 12:24)

The book of Acts opens with Jesus, immediately before ascending to the Father in heaven, promising to send the Holy Spirit upon his disciples (1:8). Ten days later that promise was fulfilled on the Day of Pentecost. Jews had gathered in Jerusalem from their homes in many countries for the annual observance of the Feast of Pentecost. On this day, the Holy Spirit fell upon the disciples of Jesus enabling them to preach the gospel in the various languages of those present (2:5-11). Peter, addressing the inhabitants of Judea and Jerusalem (2:14), powerfully testified to Jesus as the Christ. The preaching of the disciples on this day met with a tremendous response (2:41).

The spectacular events of Pentecost were followed by a period of severe testing for the followers of Jesus. During this time, the Sanhedrin commanded Peter and John not to preach any more about Jesus (4:18). In addition to facing this severe trial of persecution from without, the church was also faced with a trial from within, namely, the deceit and hypocrisy of Ananias and Sapphira (5:1-11).

The persecution against the church became so fierce that one of the first deacons, Stephen, was martyred (6:1 - 7:60). But the persecution, severe as it was, could not stop the progress of the church. Another deacon,

Philip, was blessed with great success in Samaria (8:5-25) and was used of the Lord in the conversion of a man from Ethiopia (8:26-38). One of the leading persecutors, Saul of Tarsus, was converted to the Lord as he made his way to Damascus (9:1-22). And Simon Peter was used of the Lord to achieve a major breakthrough in the progress of the gospel, namely, to lead Cornelius to the knowledge of Christ. This was a step of immense significance because Cornelius was a Gentile (10:1-48). Through this experience Simon Peter and the leaders of the church in Jerusalem came to understand that the gospel message was not for the Jews only (11:1-18).

The gospel goes to the uttermost parts of the earth
— main character, Paul (12:25 - 28:31)

In the second half the focus shifts to Paul and his missionary journeys. The first journey started at Antioch and took Paul and his companions to Seleucia (13:4), Salamis, on Cyprus (13:5), Paphos (13:6), Perga (13:13), Antioch in Pisidia (13:14), Iconium (13:51), Lystra (14:6) and Derbe (14:6). From there Paul went back to Lystra (14:8), Derbe (14:20), Lystra (14:21), Iconium (14:21), and to Antioch in Pisidia (14:21). Paul concluded this trip by stopping in Attalia (14:25) before returning to Antioch (14:26).

The first missionary journey was followed by the Jerusalem Council in which it was determined that Gentile believers did not have to submit to the Law of Moses (15:1-35).

On his second missionary journey Paul and Barnabas disagreed over whether to take John Mark along. Paul chose Silas and returned to visit the churches in Galatia, where he found Timothy in Lystra (16:1-2). It was Paul's intention on this journey to turn eastward, but he was given to understand through a vision that he was to go into Greece (16:9-10). Luke, who joined Paul at this juncture (16:10), relates the missionary party's journey to Neapolis (16:11), Philippi (16:12), Apollonia (17:1), Thessalonica (17:1), Berea (17:10), Athens (17:15), Corinth (18:1), Ephesus (18:19), Caesarea (18:22), Jerusalem (18:22) and Antioch (18:22).

The third missionary journey took Paul back to places he had visited on his first and second journeys (18:23 - 21:16).

The book of Acts concludes with Paul journeying to Jerusalem where he is arrested (21:17-37), and with the account of his transfer to Caesarea where he testifies before prominent officials (23:23 - 26:31). From Caesarea, Paul is transferred to Rome, where he is placed under house arrest. There he continues to preach to all who come to him with 'no one forbidding him' (28:30-31).

DISCUSS IT

QUESTIONS **FOR DISCUSSION**

1. Read the following: Romans 5:5; 8:9-17; 1 Corinthians 2:6-16; 3:16; 12:1-11. What functions does the Holy Spirit perform in the lives of believers?

2. Acts records the conversion of Paul. Read Philippians 3:1-16. What was the nature of his life before and after his conversion?

CHAPTER
THIRTY-SIX

THE EPISTLE OF PAUL TO THE ROMANS

ROMANS

BIBLE BOOK

THE EPISTLE OF PAUL TO THE ROMANS

Introduction

INTRODUCTION

With the book of Romans we come to the best loved of all Paul's writings. Martin Luther referred to it as 'the true masterpiece of the New Testament'.[1] And Samuel Coleridge called Romans 'the profoundest piece of writing in existence'.[2]

We also come to a book that has been wonderfully used of God. Saint Augustine, the greatest theologian during the early era of Christianity, was converted by reading a portion of Romans. It was while he was teaching this book that Martin Luther understood the gospel for the first time. That understanding became the spark that ignited the Reformation. Two centuries later, the great John Wesley was converted as a result of the message of this book. Many of the great revivals and reformations through the centuries have come about as a result of the same message being rediscovered.

Paul made three extensive missionary journeys. On the last of these he went to Corinth to collect an offering for needy believers in Palestine. It was probably during his stay there and before his departure for Jerusalem that Paul wrote to the Christians in Rome (15:26-27). If Paul did indeed write from Corinth, the date of Romans would probably be between A.D. 54 and 59.

Purpose

The *Holman Bible Dictionary* suggests that Paul wrote to the Christians in Rome for the following reasons: (1) to request their prayers as he faced the threatening situation in Jerusalem; (2) to alert them to his intended visit; (3) to acquaint them with some of his understanding of what God had done in Christ; (4) to instruct them in areas where the church faced specific problems; and (5) to enlist their support for his planned missionary venture to Spain.[3]

Structure

1. Introduction (1:1-17)
2. Doctrinal section: Salvation by faith alone (1:18 - 11:36)
   a. the need for this salvation (1:18 - 3:20)
   b. the scriptural nature of this salvation (3:21 - 4:25)
   c. the effectual nature of this salvation (5:1 - 8:39)
   d. the situation of the Jews (9:1 - 11:36)

3. Practical section: Christian service (12:1 - 15:13)
4. Conclusion (15:14 - 16:27)

Overview

Introduction (1:1-17)

Paul begins his letter by affirming his apostleship (vv. 1-5) and by explaining his reason for writing (vv. 6-15). He then states his intention to preach the gospel in Rome (1:16-17) just as he had wherever he had gone. Paul knew there would be much hostility and antagonism towards the gospel in Rome, that it was a city intoxicated with power and would look with disdain upon the idea of a Jewish Messiah dying on a cross. But Paul was not about to adjust or modify his message. He was proud of the gospel and was ready to preach it even in such a hostile environment.

Paul explains why he was so proud of the gospel. He says it is 'the power of God to salvation' (v. 16). The word 'power' is translated from the Greek word '*dunamis*', which denotes the ability to perform something. Paul was affirming, therefore, that the gospel of Christ has the ability or capacity to perform something of inestimable value, namely, saving people from their sins.

TEACHING

He also explains how the gospel has the power to save. He says, 'in it the righteousness of God is revealed' (v. 17). God requires one hundred per cent perfect right-eousness of us before he will allow us to enter into heaven. We are, of course, anything but righteous. What hope is there then for us? The gospel reveals the right-eousness we need. It declares that God has made avail-able in his Son, Jesus Christ, the very righteousness that he himself demands. This righteousness becomes ours by faith.

Doctrinal section: Salvation by faith alone (1:18 - 11:36)

a. *the need for this salvation* (1:18 - 3:20). In this sec-tion Paul works out in detail the assertion he made in the introduction, that is, God's provision of righteous-ness in and through his Son. He does so by first show-ing that all without exception need this righteousness. The Gentiles needed it because they had suppressed the knowledge of God they had received from nature and their own consciences (1:18-32). The Jews needed it because they had failed to obey the very law of God they professed to revere (2:1 - 3:8). Paul concludes, then, that both Jews and Greeks were 'all under sin' (3:9) and 'all have sinned and fall short of the glory of God' (3:23).

b. *the scriptural nature of this salvation* (3:21 - 4:25). Here Paul presents the doctrine of justification. Justifi-cation is the opposite of condemnation. It is God de-claring the sinner to be just or guiltless. How is it possible for God to do such a thing? Through Christ! Christ lived in perfect obedience to the law of God throughout his life. He had, therefore, the righteousness we need. On the cross, Christ took the punishment for all who believe in him. To be justified means we receive Christ's righteousness while he received our sin (2 Cor. 5:21).

Paul shows his readers that he was not teaching something new and different, that this was in fact the very same way both Abraham and David were saved in the Old Testament (4:1-25).

c. *the effectual nature of this salvation* (5:1 - 8:39). The salvation provided by Christ creates these marvellous benefits: peace (5:1), holiness (6:22), spiritual joy (7:22) and perseverance in the faith (8:33-39).

d. *the situation of the Jews* (9:1 - 11:36). In this section Paul grapples with this profound question: Where did his message of salvation leave the Jews? They believed themselves to be the true people of God although most of them had rejected Jesus. Paul answers this question by affirming that salvation was never just a matter of nationality. Being a Jew had never meant that one was automatically saved (9:6). Salvation in the Old Testament era had always been a matter of God's mercy bringing people to faith in the coming Christ. Although many of the Jews had indeed rejected Christ, Paul rejoiced in this: that the same mercy of God would still bring many Jews to true faith.

Practical section: Christian service (12:1 - 15:13)

Having laid out for his readers the doctrine of salvation by the grace of God, in this section Paul turns to this question: How should God's people live in the light of all he did to save them? As far as the apostle was concerned there was only one possible answer: living lives of dedicated obedience. This is why he calls service to God 'reasonable' (12:1). It is the only logical conclusion for those who have been saved by grace. *The Open Bible* says: 'A changed life is not a condition for salvation, but it should be the natural outcome of saving faith.'⁴

Paul proceeds from this point to call the Romans to function as responsible members of the church, the body of Christ (12:3-21), to fulfil their obligations to the state (13:1-7), to make love supreme in their lives (13:8-14), and to nurture each other in the fellowship of the church, paying special attention to the weaker members (14:1 - 15:13).

Conclusion (15:14 - 16:27)

Paul concluded his letter by summarizing his plans (15:14-33), by commending Phoebe (16:1-2) and by extending greetings to individual members of the church (16:3-24). Even while Paul was engaged in practical matters, the glorious gospel of Christ was never far from his mind. In his closing words, he returns to that theme by offering heartfelt praise to God for fulfilling his promises by sending Christ (16:25-27).

QUESTIONS FOR DISCUSSION

1. Read Paul's statement about justification by faith in Galatians 2:16. What is the context of this statement? Who had compromised on this doctrine by his behaviour? How did Paul respond?

2. Read James 2:14-26. Do good works secure our justification or are they the result of it?

CHAPTER
THIRTY-SEVEN

THE FIRST
EPISTLE OF
PAUL TO THE
CORINTHIANS

BIBLE BOOK

THE FIRST EPISTLE OF PAUL TO THE CORINTHIANS

Introduction

INTRODUCTION

Situated on a narrow strip of land, only four miles across, Corinth was the major city of Greece. A strategic centre of commerce by land and sea, it was a city that was synonymous with immorality and debauchery, so much so that even the popular religions had incorporated sexual practices. The most prominent temple in this city of temples was the Temple of Aphrodite, the goddess of love. This cult offered worshippers 1,000 prostitutes.

On his second missionary journey the apostle Paul spent eighteen months in Corinth. There he made tents with Aquila and Priscilla and succeeded in starting a church (Acts 18). This took place in the years A.D. 51 and 52.

After leaving Corinth, Paul went to Ephesus, Jerusalem and Antioch of Syria. He then returned to Ephesus for a two-year ministry. During this time, Paul became aware of serious problems in the church of Corinth and began corresponding with the members.

Purpose

The problems of the Corinthian Church were so great that Paul found it necessary to write four letters. The first, referred to in 1 Corinthians 5:9, was lost. The second is the letter we know as 1 Corinthians. The third was the 'letter of tears' which Paul mentions in 2 Corinthians 2:4. This letter was also lost. The fourth is 2 Corinthians.

The first of these letters evidently consisted of a very strong rebuke to the church members for their careless living. It did not put an end to the problem, but it did prompt a return letter from the Corinthians in which they posed several questions. 1 Corinthians is Paul's response to this return letter. It is another impassioned plea for the church to deal decisively with their problems, and it is the wise response of his pastor's heart to the questions that they had raised.

Structure

Introduction (1:1-9)
1. Paul deals with the problems of the church (1:10 - 6:20)
    a. The problem of division (1:10 - 4:21)
    b. The problem of worldliness (5:1 - 6:20)
2. Paul answers the questions of the church (7:1 - 16:4)
    a. Regarding marriage (7:1-40)
    b. Regarding meat sacrificed to idols (8:1 - 11:1)
    c. Regarding spiritual gifts (11:2 - 14:40)

Overview

Introduction (1:1-9)

Paul begins by reminding the Corinthians of the truth about himself (1:1) and the truth about themselves (1:2,4-9). He was an apostle of Jesus Christ, and was, therefore, in position to deal with their problems and questions. They were recipients of God's gracious salvation, and should, therefore, be very anxious to live up to their calling.

Paul deals with the problems of the church (1:10 - 6:20)

a. *The problem of division* (1:10 - 4:21). Paul had received a report (1:10) that the members of the church were divided into various personality cults. Some professed to be followers of Paul, some of Apollos, some of Cephas (Simon Peter), and some of Christ (1:12). Those in the latter group would seem to be correct, but they were not. Essentially, these 'Christ-boasters' were claiming that Christ belonged exclusively to them.

TEACHING

Paul located the source of this division in the Corinthians' infatuation with worldly wisdom and in a fundamental misunderstanding of the gospel ministry. He sought to break down the former by reminding them that they were not saved by human wisdom (1:18-31), and that his preaching among them had not featured human wisdom (2:1-5). He attacked the latter by giving them a detailed description of a genuine ministry (3:1 - 4:21). While he did not want the Corinthians to stop prizing ministers of the gospel, he did want them to stop exalting preachers in undue measure.

b. *The problem of worldliness* (5:1 - 6:20). Having treated the problem of disunity, Paul turns to grapple with a particularly distasteful problem that had cropped up. Paul summarizes it in these words: 'a man has his father's wife' (5:1). The wording suggests the member was committing immorality, not with his own mother, but rather with his stepmother. Leon Morris writes: 'Whether it means that the offender had seduced his stepmother, or that she was divorced from his father, or that the father had died, leaving her a widow, is not clear. What is quite clear is that an illicit union of a particularly unsavoury kind had been contracted.'[1]

Even more disturbing to Paul was the indifference of the church to this situation (5:2). He called upon the church to discipline the offending member (5:3-9), remembering that heaven is a pure place (6:9-11) and that they themselves had been dramatically changed (6:11).

Paul answers the questions of the church (7:1 - 16:4)

a. *Regarding marriage* (7:1-40). Some of the Corinthians, perhaps seeking to withstand the prevalent sexual immorality of their city, were in danger of going to the opposite extreme by arguing that Christians should avoid all sexual relations. They evidently believed single Christians should not consider marriage and that those who were married should either avoid sexual relations or get a divorce. Paul responded by affirming that while the single life is good (7:1-9), marriage is natural (7:10-24).

b. *Regarding meat sacrificed to idols* (8:1 - 11:1). In Corinth meat sacrifices were an essential part of idol worship. While Christians did not make these sacrifices they could not avoid coming into contact with this meat. Part of it was consumed by the offering. Part was given as payment to the priests, and part was kept by the worshipper. The priests, not being able to use all the meat they received, sold most of it to the markets. When a Christian went to buy meat, he had no way of knowing whether it had been used in idol worship. Paul dealt with this issue by urging the Christians who felt free to eat this meat to be willing to forego it for the sake of those who did not feel the same freedom.

c. *Regarding worship* (11:2 - 14:40). The Corinthians had asked Paul about the role of women in worship, the observance of the Lord's Supper and spiritual gifts. Paul gave instructions on each of these matters. In the midst of his discussion of spiritual gifts, he called for a spirit of love in words that constitute one of the mountain-peak chapters of the Bible (13:1-13). With that in place he warns the church to be especially on guard against abuse of the gift of tongues (14:1-40).

d. *Regarding the resurrection* (15:1-58). Paul was shocked that some of the Corinthians had doubts about this vital doctrine. He affirmed the resurrection of Christ as an indispensable part of the gospel (15:1-4) and an indisputable fact of history (15:5-11), and insisted that it guarantees the resurrection unto eternal glory of all those who belong to Christ (15:20-58).

e. *Regarding financial matters* (16:1-4). Here Paul appeals for the Corinthians to collect money for the church in Jerusalem, which was in dire straits because of persecution and famine.

Conclusion (16:5-24)

Paul brings his letter to a close by informing the Corinthians of his plans (16:5-12), by encouraging the Corinthians to be faithful and loving (16:13-14), by expressing thanks for certain individuals in the church (16:15-18), by sharing greetings from others (16:19-20)

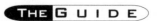

and by pronouncing a curse on all those who do not love Christ (16:21-24).

QUESTIONS FOR DISCUSSION

DISCUSS IT

1. *Paul urged the Corinthians to be united. Read Psalm 133:1; Romans 12:16; 14:19; Romans 15:5; 2 Corinthians 13:11; Ephesians 4:3; Philippians 1:27; 2:5-11; 3:16; 1 Peter 3:8. What incentives do Christians have for being united? What practical steps can they take to that end?*

2. *1 Corinthians 12 contains a list of spiritual gifts. Read Romans 12:6-8; Ephesians 4:7-16. How do you explain the lack of uniformity in these lists?*

3. *1 Corinthians 15 emphasizes the resurrection of Christ. Read Romans 1:4. What does the resurrection of Christ prove? Read Romans 4:25. What does it provide? Read Romans 8:11. What does it guarantee?*

CHAPTER
THIRTY-EIGHT

THE SECOND EPISTLE OF PAUL TO THE CORINTHIANS

2 CORINTHIANS

THE SECOND EPISTLE OF PAUL TO THE CORINTHIANS

Introduction

In the conclusion of 1 Corinthians we find Paul anticipating Timothy making a visit to the church of Corinth (1 Cor. 16:10). That visit apparently took place and yielded the bad news of considerable opposition to the apostle. Paul responded to this report by visiting Corinth himself. His visit, while not reported in the book of Acts, can be inferred from Paul's own statements (2 Cor. 2:1; 12:14; 13:1-2). This visit is known as 'the painful visit' because it evidently featured an ugly incident in which one of the congregation insulted Paul while the other members sat idly by.

After returning to Ephesus, Paul sorrowfully wrote to the church and sent the 'letter of tears' with Titus. In this letter, which we do not possess, the apostle called the church to discipline the man who had opposed him. Paul was so eager to receive Titus' report on the reception of this letter that he left Ephesus and went first to Troas (2:12) and then to Macedonia to meet him

(7:6,13). He was greatly relieved to learn that most of the Corinthians had repented of their opposition, and the man who so vigorously opposed Paul had been disciplined by the congregation and had repented. While in Macedonia, Paul wrote 2 Corinthians and dispatched Titus and another brother (12:18) to carry it to Corinth. The date of this writing was A.D. 56.

Purposes

Paul wrote 2 Corinthians for these reasons:

1. To express his delight at the Corinthians' repentance
2. To caution them not to be too severe with the chief offender
3. To clear up any remaining doubts about his calling and his authority as an apostle
4. To instruct them regarding the offering for the saints in Jerusalem.

Structure

Introduction (1:1-11)
1. Paul explains his ministry (1:12 - 7:16)
2. Paul appeals for generous giving (8:1 - 9:15)
3. Paul defends his apostleship (10:1 - 12:13)
4. Paul announces his plans (12:14 - 13:10)
Conclusion (13:11-14)

Overview

Introduction (1:1-11)

Paul begins his letter by identifying himself as an apostle of Christ (v. 1) and by offering praise to God for comforting him in the midst of affliction (vv. 3-7) and for delivering him from affliction (vv. 8-11).

Paul explains his ministry (1:12 - 7:16)

The apostle begins this section by dealing with a misunderstanding that had arisen about him and his ministry. He had intended to visit the Corinthians on his way into Macedonia and on his way back (1:15-17). The developments in the church had caused him to send a letter instead (2:4,9).

This change of plans served to fuel the opposition of his critics in Corinth. They argued that it proved him to be unreliable and fickle (1:17). Paul responds by assuring the Corinthians that his change of plans was to spare them and himself additional pain (1:23; 2:1-2).

This misunderstanding opened the door for Paul to give his readers the following proofs that he was indeed a genuine minister of Christ. His ministry was confirmed by:

1. the faith of the Corinthians themselves (3:1-3)
2. its glorious and liberating nature (3:4-18)

TEACHING

3. how and what Paul had preached (4:1-7)
4. his willingness to suffer hardship (4:8 - 5:8)

Paul's sufferings were so many and so severe that one cannot help but ask how he could so willingly endure them. Paul answers this question by pointing to the following:

1. the ongoing renewal of his inner man (4:16)
2. the transforming power of looking at things from the perspective of eternity (4:17-18)
3. the confident expectation of a new body (5:1-8)
4. the consuming desire to please the Lord (5:9)
5. the keen awareness of accountability to the Lord (5:10-11)
6. the constraint of Christ's love (5:12-16)
7. gratitude for redemption (5:17-21)

After stating the evidences and motivations of his ministry, Paul called upon his readers to respond by being reconciled to him (6:11-13; 7:2-16) and by being separated from the world (6:14 - 7:1).

Paul appeals for generous giving (8:1 - 9:15)

While 2 Corinthians is the most personal and biographical of all the letters Paul wrote, it is not exclusively about Paul and his ministry. Paul was far too concerned about others for that. He turns in this section, then, to call upon the Corinthians to give generously to the collection he was receiving for the impoverished saints in

Jerusalem. He supplies motivation for the Corinthians to support this offering by citing the examples of the Macedonians (8:1-5) and the Lord Jesus Christ (8:9). He also assures them that their gifts would demonstrate maturity and love (8:6,8), would fulfill their obligations (8:10-11), would not unduly burden them (8:12-15) and would be handled honestly (8:20-21). Later on, he assures them that through their gifts they would be investing in a great spiritual harvest (9:6-8).

Paul defends his apostleship (10:1 - 12:13)

Although most of the Corinthians had turned from their opposition to him, Paul knew some were persisting in it. He first deals with the mistaken perception these critics had of him, namely, that he did not have an authoritative, appealing presence (10:1) and that he 'walked according to the flesh', that is, was lacking in spirituality (10:2). Paul answers these charges by reminding the Corinthians that spirituality is not a matter of outward appearances. Christians are fighting in a spiritual war that demands spiritual weapons (10:3-5).

From that point he proceeds to show them that spirituality is not a matter of boasting (10:13-18). If the Corinthians were going to judge spirituality on the basis of boasting, they would have to regard Paul as superior to all other

TEACHING

teachers because he had more to boast about than they. Paul reminds the Corinthians that: (1) he had travelled as great a distance as others to reach them; (2) he was the first to reach them; (3) he had gone even greater distances to preach in regions beyond Corinth; (4) it is not how far a man travels but what he preaches that matters. After showing the Corinthians that he had as much to boast about as others, Paul says all such boasting is pointless. It is the Lord who keeps the records, and the true teacher is not necessarily the most popular with the people but rather the one who enjoys God's approval (10:17-18).

To these arguments Paul adds a list of proofs of his apostleship: the sufferings he had endured (11:16-33), the revelations he had been granted (12:1-10) and the signs he had performed (12:11-13).

Paul announces his plans (12:14 - 13:10)

Paul is now planning to visit the Corinthians again. His pledge is that he will come to them in love and for their edification (12:14-19). His plea is for them to lay aside their sinful living so that his visit with them will be pleasant and will not require him to exercise his authority as an apostle (13:2-4).

Conclusion (13:11-14)

Paul ends his letter with a series of brief exhortations (13:11), greetings (13:13) and a benediction (13:14).

DISCUSS IT

1. Paul called the Corinthians to be separated from the world (6:11-18). Read Matthew 5:14; Galatians 6:14; Titus 2:12; James 1:27. How is the Christian to relate to the world? Read 1 Corinthians 3:19; 2 Timothy 4:10; James 4:4; 2 Peter 1:4; 1 John 2:15-17. What dangers does the world present to the Christian?

2. Paul urged the Corinthians to give generously to the work of the Lord. Read Matthew 6:1-4; Luke 21:1-4; 1 Corinthians 16:1-2. What do these passages teach us about giving?

CHAPTER
THIRTY-NINE

THE EPISTLE OF PAUL TO THE GALATIANS

BIBLE BOOK

THE EPISTLE OF PAUL TO THE GALATIANS

Introduction

The epistle to the Galatians was written by the apostle Paul to the churches he had started on his first missionary journey. The fact that he does not mention the Jerusalem Council, which would have had a tremendous bearing on the issue with which he was dealing, indicates that he wrote before it was convened. A date of A.D. 49 is widely accepted for Galatians, making it the first of Paul's letters.

Purposes

Galatians is like no other letter Paul wrote. The early Christian leader Jerome had this to say about it: 'When I read Paul, I can hear thunder.'[1] Timothy George says: 'It is the most passionate thing he (Paul) wrote. It's the only letter in which he doesn't have a kind of friendly greeting at the beginning. He jumped in with both fists flying.'[2]

What so provoked the apostle? The Galatians were allowing themselves to be led astray by false teachers. These men, while professing to be Christians, were essentially trying to make Christianity an extension of Judaism. They were teaching that faith in Christ was not sufficient, that it was necessary for those who had embraced Christ to submit to the Jewish rite of circumcision as well as to other regulations in the law of Moses. They were teaching salvation by faith plus works.

Paul was astonished that the Galatians seemed to be confused on this point. If salvation is by grace, it cannot be by works. If it is by works, it cannot be by grace. The one nullifies the other.

Structure

1. The issue of authority — Paul defends his apostleship (1:1 - 2:10)
   a. Introduction: Paul answers the charge that he was not really an apostle (1:1-5)
   b. Anathema: Paul answers the charge that he was a popularity seeker who would do anything to get a following (1:6-10)
   c. Testimony of conversion: Paul answers the charge that his gospel was the product of human speculation (1:11-24)
   d. Account of trip to Jerusalem: Paul answers the charge that his gospel was out of step with the Jewish leaders (2:1-10)

2. The issue of salvation — Paul defends his gospel (2:11 - 5:12)
   a. Paul expounds the truth of the gospel (2:11-21)
   b. Paul exposes the folly of the Galatians (3:1 - 5:12)

3. The issue of holiness — Paul defends the gospel against licence (5:13 - 6:10)
   a. the law of love does not permit the Christian to live licentiously (5:13-15,26; 6:1-10)
   b. the Holy Spirit does not permit the Christian to live licentiously (5:16-26)

Conclusion (6:11-18)

Overview

The issue of authority — Paul defends his apostleship (1:1 - 2:10)

It was not mere formality that caused Paul to identify himself so decisively as an apostle in the opening words of his letter. The Judaizers knew they could not be successful in promulgating their views until they discredited the authority of Paul. Paul's very first words drove to the heart of this issue. He not only identifies himself as an apostle but also claims that his apostleship was from the Lord himself. It is interesting that Paul proceeds to refer to those who were with him as 'brethren' (1:2), but he reserves the title 'apostle' for himself.

Having identified himself as an apostle, Paul expresses his amazement that the Galatians were turning away from his gospel to embrace a gospel that was no gospel at all (1:6-7). To this he adds an anathema (curse) upon all those who preach 'any other gospel' (1:8). This curse was universal in scope (Paul even included himself) and deliberate (it is repeated) (1:8-9). Paul's point is clear. If he were a popularity seeker, he would not hurl out such an anathema.

If we find Paul's anathema to be unnerving, it is because we do not share his passion for the gospel of Christ that alone can save sinners from eternal condemnation. We will never share this passion if we do not understand the next point Paul makes, namely, the gospel is God's plan. It is not a mere human invention but rather a divine revelation (1:11-12). Paul's conversion as well as his post-conversion activities proved that the gospel had been divinely revealed to him (1:13-24). One of those activities was a trip to Jerusalem (well after Paul's conversion) in which Paul's gospel was endorsed by the leaders there (1:18-24).

John R. W. Stott offers this summary statement regarding Paul: 'The fanaticism of his pre-conversion career, the divine initiative in his conversion, and his almost total isolation from the Jerusalem church leaders afterwards combined to demonstrate that his message was not from man but from God.'[3]

The issue of salvation — Paul defends his gospel (2:11 - 5:12)

In this section Paul uses the compromise of his fellow-apostle, Peter, to clearly and powerfully affirm the very core of the gospel, that is, sinners are justified before God by faith alone in Christ alone and not by works (2:16).

Paul knew his position led his critics to raise this objection: 'Paul, your doctrine of justification through faith alone is highly dangerous. It fatally weakens a man's sense of moral responsibility. If he can be accepted by God through faith without any necessity of doing good works, he is actually encouraged to break the law. You are, therefore, making Christ the cause of men's sins' (2:17).

Paul responds to this objection by affirming that the one who is justified by faith is also united or joined to Christ. He was crucified with Christ and Christ now lives in him and gives him a desire for holiness.

In the remaining portion of this section, Paul exposes the folly of the Galatians (3:1 - 5:12). He turns his attention from the false teachers who were troubling them to those who were allowing themselves to be troubled. He asserts that through heeding these false teachers, the Galatians were: (1) denying their own experience (3:1-5); (2) denying the Scriptures (3:6-9); (3) misconstruing the very essence of Christ's death (3:13-14); (4) misconstruing the nature and purpose of the law (3:15-29); (5) trading freedom for bondage (4:1-11); (6) disparaging Paul's ministry (4:12-20); and (7) failing to hear the message of the law (4:21-31).

Paul closes this section by exhorting the Galatians to faithfulness (5:1-12).

The issue of holiness — Paul defends the gospel against licence (5:13 - 6:10)

Because the Judaizers had distorted Paul's doctrine by asserting that it led people to believe they could live as they pleased, Paul devotes the last part of his letter to denying this. He argues that the Christian's love for God and for his fellow-man forbids him to violate the laws of God. Paul does not say if we have love, we can violate the law, but rather if we love, we shall keep the law.

Paul also called the Galatians to walk in the Spirit (5:16), knowing that this would preclude them from walking in sin. Walking in the Spirit means we understand the ugliness of what the flesh produces (5:19-21), we understand the beauty of what the Spirit produces (5:22-23), we crucify the desires of the flesh (5:24-26), we walk in concern for our brothers and sisters in Christ (6:1-10).

Conclusion (6:11-18)

Paul concludes his letter by contrasting the motives of the false teachers (6:11-13) with his own (6:14-15) and by asking God's blessings on those who walk in the right way (6:16-18).

DISCUSS IT

1. Read Romans 1:16-17. Why was Paul so passionate about the gospel of Christ?

2. Paul's list of the fruit of the Spirit (5:22-23) reminds us of Jesus' words in John 15:1-8. Is fruit-bearing inevitable for the believer? Read also Matthew 13:23.

THE GUIDE

CHAPTER FORTY

THE EPISTLE OF PAUL TO THE EPHESIANS

BIBLE BOOK

THE EPISTLE OF PAUL TO THE EPHESIANS

Introduction

INTRODUCTION

The letter to the Ephesians is the first of Paul's prison epistles (the others are Philippians, Colossians and Philemon). It is generally considered to have been written by the apostle during his first Roman imprisonment in A.D. 60-62. Paul makes reference to his imprisonment in verses 3:1; 4:1; and 6:20.

Although Paul addresses himself to 'the saints who are in Ephesus' (1:1), some think this letter was intended for all of Paul's churches in Asia Minor. Proponents of this view argue that Paul addressed himself to the Ephesians because their city was the foremost of the area. They cite the following:

1. Paul deals with no specific problem as he did when he was writing to a particular church.

2. There is an absence of terms of endearment, a fact which seems strange in light of the amount of time Paul spent in the city of Ephesus.

Purpose

Whether Paul intended his letter for Ephesus only or for other churches as well, his purposes in writing are evident. He wanted to remind his readers of their glorious position in and through Christ and to encourage them to live in accordance with their high position.

Structure

Salutation (1:1-2)

1. The Christian sitting in heavenly places (1:3 - 3:21)
   a. A hymn of praise for spiritual blessings (1:3-14)
   b. A prayer for understanding (1:15-23)
   c. A celebration of spiritual resurrection (2:1-10)
   d. A celebration of reconciliation (2:11-22)
   e. The revelation of a mystery (3:1-13)
   f. Another prayer for understanding (3:14-21)

2. The Christian walking in strategic places (4:1 - 6:9)
   a. The church (4:1-16)
   b. The world (4:17 - 5:21)
   c. The home (5:22 - 6:9)

3. The Christian standing in warfare (6:10-20)

Conclusion (6:21-24)

Overview

Salutation (1:1-2)

Paul begins by identifying himself as an apostle of Christ and by asking God to bestow grace and peace on his readers.

The Christian sitting in heavenly places (1:3 - 3:21)

A hymn of praise for spiritual blessings (1:3-14). In this section, the apostle mentions nine spiritual blessings enjoyed by each and every child of God. We have been chosen (1:4), adopted (1:5), accepted (1:6), redeemed (1:7), forgiven (1:7-8), given insight into God's plan for us (1:9-10), given an inheritance (1:11-12), sealed with the Spirit (1:13), and given the Holy Spirit as a guarantee of our inheritance (1:14).

All of these riches have come to us through none other than the Lord Jesus Christ himself. In the first fourteen verses of this chapter, we find a name, title or pronoun for Christ appearing fifteen times. And the phrases 'in Christ' or 'in him' appear eleven times.

A prayer for understanding (1:15-23). Just as it is possible for us to be materially rich and not realize it, so it is possible for Christians to not realize how rich they are spiritually. Paul prays,

TEACHING

therefore, for his readers to understand the hope of the Lord's calling (1:18), the glory of his inheritance (1:18) and the greatness of his power (1:19-23).

A celebration of spiritual resurrection (2:1-10). Every Christian was in a state of spiritual deadness when God graciously came to him and granted him spiritual life. Salvation is entirely a matter of God's grace.

A celebration of reconciliation (2:11-22). In addition to being raised from spiritual deadness, believing Jews and Gentiles have been reconciled to God and to each other.

The revelation of a mystery (3:1-13). The reconciliation of Jews and Gentiles opened the door for the apostle to discuss a mystery (a truth that would have remained unknown had God not revealed it), namely, 'that the Gentiles should be fellow heirs, of the same body, and partakers of his promise in Christ through the gospel...' (3:6).

Another prayer for understanding (3:14-21). Paul offers yet another prayer in these verses. He asks the Lord to: (1) strengthen his readers with his might; (2) give them understanding of the greatness of Christ's love; (3) fill them with the fulness of God.

The Christian walking in strategic places (4:1 - 6:9)

In the last half of his letter the apostle turns from the doctrinal to the practical. The key word in this section is 'walk' (4:1,17; 5:2,8,15). This word refers to the Christian's manner of life or conduct. Paul focuses on the walk of the Christian in three vital areas.

The church (4:1-16). Christians are to walk in the church by showing sympathy towards each other (4:2), by maintaining unity among themselves (4:3-6), by understanding their diversity (4:7-12) and by striving towards maturity (4:13-16).

The world (4:17 - 5:21). The Christian is to walk in this world in such a way as to reveal the difference Christ has made in his life. He is not to walk as others do (4:17-21) or as he himself once did (4:22-32). Instead he is to walk as God himself walks, that is, in love and in light (5:1-14). Furthermore, he is to walk carefully and wisely in this world by redeeming the time, by understanding the will of the Lord and by being filled with the Holy Spirit (5:15-21).

The home (5:22 - 6:9). Paul's instructions regarding family living encompass three relationships: husband-wife (5:22-33), parent-child (6:1-4) and master-servant (6:5-9). He calls upon wives to be submissive (5:22-24), husbands to be loving (5:25-33), children to be obedient (6:1-3), parents to be understanding in discipline (6:4), servants to work willingly (6:5-8) and masters to be kind and understanding (6:9).

The Christian standing in warfare (6:10-20)

Christians will not be able to carry out their responsibilities until they understand that they are engaged in a great spiritual warfare against many forces of darkness (6:12). To fight successfully, they must be covered with the armour that God himself provides. This armour consists of:

1. the girdle of truth — settled in our convictions
2. the breastplate of righteousness — the righteousness provided by God in and through Christ. We put this on by reminding ourselves of it.
3. the gospel shoes — standing firmly on the peace the gospel provides
4. the shield of faith — relying on God and his promises
5. the helmet of salvation — fortifying our minds with God's promises regarding the future
6. the sword of the Spirit — using the Word of God to thwart Satan's attacks

Conclusion (6:21-24)

The apostle closes his letter by informing his readers of the coming of Tychicus (6:21-22) and by again expressing his desire for the church to be blessed (6:23-24).

QUESTIONS FOR DISCUSSION

DISCUSS IT

1. Read 2 Corinthians 5:7; Galatians 5:16,25; Colossians 1:10; 2:6; 1 John 1:7; 2:6; 2 John 6; 3 John 3-4. What do these verses teach us about the walk of the believer?

2. Read 2 Timothy 2:1-6 for more about the Christian life as a warfare. What was necessary for Timothy to be a good soldier? What other figures does Paul use to illustrate the Christian life?

THE GUIDE

CHAPTER
FORTY-ONE

THE EPISTLE OF PAUL TO THE PHILIPPIANS

BIBLE BOOK

THE EPISTLE OF PAUL TO THE PHILIPPIANS

Introduction

Philippians, the second of Paul's prison epistles, was written by the apostle to the church he started in Philippi on his second missionary journey (Acts 16:6-40). Because of his references to 'the palace guard' (1:13) and 'Caesar's household' (4:22), the traditional position is that Paul wrote Philippians during the Roman imprisonment described in Acts 28. The date of Paul's writing is usually placed between A.D. 61 and 64.

Purpose

Paul had the following purposes in writing to the Philippians:

1. to report on his circumstances
2. to express appreciation for their concern for him and a gift they had sent to him by Epaphroditus
3. to assure them that Epaphroditus, who became ill while with Paul, had ministered

satisfactorily to him and was now well enough to return to them

4. to urge them to fulfill various duties
5. to warn them about the ever-present danger of false teachers

In the midst of all these practical concerns, the apostle continually expresses his abounding joy in Christ. The words 'joy' and 'rejoice' appear sixteen times in this brief letter, and references to Christ (including pronouns) are found 61 times in its 104 verses. It is obvious that Christ, not circumstances, was the source of Paul's joy.

Structure

Introduction (1:1-2)
1. Thanksgiving (1:3-25)
2. Appeal for unity (1:27 - 2:30)
3. Warning about false teachers (3:1 - 4:1)
4. Final exhortations (4:2-20)
Conclusion (4:21-23)

Overview

Introduction (1:1-2)

Paul includes Timothy in his greeting because the latter was with him at the time of writing and shared

Paul's appreciation and concern for the Philippians. Timothy may very well have penned the words of this letter as the apostle dictated them.

Thanksgiving (1:3-25)

Paul rejoiced in the bond of fellowship he enjoyed with the Philippians who had loved him from 'the first day until now' (1:5). He assured the Philippians of his grateful remembrances of them (1:3) and his joyful prayers for them (1:4). The apostle also expressed his confidence that the God who had created the spirit of concern reflected by the Philippians would continue working in them. Salvation is God's work, and he never stops before the work is done.

Paul also rejoiced in his own imprisonment because he could see that God was using it for the furtherance of the gospel (1:12-18). How this man loved the gospel and yearned to see it advance! His zeal rebukes us for our own lukewarm interest.

The apostle was not sure what the outcome of his imprisonment would be. He felt confident that he would be released to continue his ministry (1:25), but also knew there was the distinct possibility that he would be executed (1:20). Even the prospect of death could not diminish his joy. It would only give him one more way to magnify the Christ he loved (1:20), and it would bring great personal gain to him.

Appeal for unity (1:27 - 2:30)

This appeal falls into two major parts. Firstly, Paul says the outer life of the church demands unity (1:27-30). Proclaiming the gospel to an unbelieving world is no easy task. There are adversaries who can be very terrifying (1:28). The challenge requires the church to 'stand fast in one spirit' and to strive together 'for the faith of the gospel' (1:27). It is never pleasant to face the hostility of an unbelieving world, but that hostility gives us the consolation that we are indeed the children of God (1:28-30).

Secondly, Paul says the inner life of the church demands unity (2:1-11). He first gives incentives for unity in the fellowship of the church (2:1-2) and the requirements for that unity, that is, humbling self and helping others (2:3-4).

He powerfully drives home this appeal by citing the example of the Lord Jesus Christ, who did not consider his glory something that he had to cling to at all costs, but willingly laid it aside and stooped so low as to take our humanity. As a man, Jesus humbled himself even to the point that he died on the cross. Because Christ did this so willingly, God has highly exalted him (2:5-11). If we humble ourselves, God will also exalt us in due time.

Paul further encourages the Philippians to humility by citing the service of Timothy and Epaphroditus (2:19-30).

Warning about false teachers (3:1 - 4:1)

The apostle warns his readers of the Judaizers who taught that faith in Christ was not enough for salvation, that one must also keep the law of Moses (3:1-2). In his early years, Paul himself assumed that he could produce the righteousness God demanded. For a long time he convinced himself that he was well on the way to accomplishing this very thing. In addition to what his parents had given him (circumcision and a noble birth — 3:5), he had attained several things through his own efforts (recognition as a Pharisee, zealousness, legal rectitude — 3:5-6).

Paul came to see that all he attained was of no avail. He came to understand that he was only keeping the law outwardly, whereas God's demand for perfect righteousness included even internal desires (see Rom. 7:7-11). When he saw that he had failed to live up to God's perfect standard, he was driven to despair. But then, by the grace of God, he saw something else, namely, that God himself had provided the righteousness he requires, a righteousness that also becomes ours by faith.

After having received Christ's righteousness, Paul found himself longing to know Christ intimately (3:10-14). What was necessary to realize such intimate knowledge? Firstly, there had to be a dissatisfaction with what he had so far attained in this area (3:12). Secondly, there had to be a single-minded zeal that forgot the past and pressed on with dogged determination towards the goal (3:13-14).

Closing words (4:2-20)

This section consists of words of exhortation (4:2-9) and a personal testimony from Paul (4:10-19). His exhortations were directed to two women in the church (4:2) and to the church in general (2:4-9). With regard to the latter, Paul urges the Philippians to rejoice in the Lord (4:4), to be gentle and kind (4:5), to trust and pray (4:6-7), to think about the right things (4:8) and to obey the Word of God (4:9).

After stressing these things, the apostle shifts to personal gratitude for the caring ministry of the Philippians (4:10,16-18). While he was grateful for their ministry, he did not depend on it. He had taught himself to be content even if there was no support from others. How did Paul teach himself contentment? It was by drawing on the sufficiency of Christ for every situation (4:13).

Conclusion (4:21-23)

Paul closes his letter with greetings and a blessing.

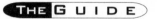

DISCUSS IT

QUESTIONS FOR DISCUSSION

1. Read Psalm 51; Jeremiah 15:16; Luke 10:17-20; 1 Peter 1:3-9. What reasons do Christians have to rejoice?

2. Read Isaiah 45:23-25. When all bow before Christ, what will they say? Will all those who bow share the same destiny?

CHAPTER
FORTY-TWO

THE EPISTLE OF PAUL TO THE COLOSSIANS

COLOSSIANS

BIBLE BOOK

THE EPISTLE OF PAUL TO THE COLOSSIANS

Introduction

INTRODUCTION

The letter to the Colossians was written by the apostle Paul to the church that had been established there. While Paul never visited this church (1:4-8; 2:1), he had a deep interest in the Lord's work wherever it was found. His interest in the church had to be heightened by the fact that it had been started by Epaphras (1:7) who may have come to faith during Paul's ministry in Ephesus (100 miles west of Colosse).

Colossians is the third of Paul's prison epistles. Many think it was written during his first Roman imprisonment in A.D. 60 or 61. During this time Paul received a visit from Epaphras with a report of the church's progress and of a particular menace it was then facing.

The letter to the Colossians is strikingly similar to Ephesians. The two epistles have the same basic division (first half doctrinal, second half practical), and they cover many of the same themes. But there are differences. While Ephesians focuses on the church of Christ, Colossians focuses on the Christ of the church.

We might say the former focuses on the body, while the latter focuses on the head.

Purpose

Paul wrote the Colossians to urge his readers to continue in the faith (1:23; 2:6). This exhortation was necessary because of a dangerous heresy that had crept into the church. This heresy was evidently a synthesis of Jewish practices and pagan speculation. Geoffrey Wilson explains: 'The Jewish element in this false teaching called for Gentile observance of the ritual requirements of the law ... while its pagan element encouraged the worship of angelic intermediaries ... and enjoined an asceticism which in its severe treatment of the body went beyond the law's demands...'[1]

The advocates of these teachings were attacking the sufficiency and the supremacy of the Lord Jesus Christ. They were essentially arguing that Christ was not a complete Saviour, and that it was necessary to follow their rules and regulations to attain fulness and happiness. To them Christ was merely one of a whole series of steps to God.

Structure

1. The personal section (1:1-14)
   a. Paul greets the church (1:1-2)
   b. Paul expresses thanks to God for the church (1:3-8)

TEACHING

Overview

The personal section (1:1-14)

Paul greets the church (1:1-2). Paul follows his usual pattern in greeting the Colossians. He identifies himself as an apostle (v. 1) and wishes them grace and peace (v. 2).

Paul expresses thanks to God for the church (1:3-8). Paul was thankful for the faith (v. 4), the love (v. 4) and the hope of the church (v. 5). He was also thankful for the work of the gospel in them (vv. 6-8).

Paul prays for the church (1:9-14). Each of Paul's two petitions is signalled by the word 'that' in the New King James Version:

1. That they would be filled with the knowledge of God's will (v. 9)
2. That they would have a walk worthy of the Lord and pleasing to him (vv. 10-11)

To have a walk worthy of the Lord is: (a) to be fruitful, that is, to maintain good works; (b) to steadily increase in the knowledge of God; (c) to draw our strength from him, strength that will be reflected in patiently and joyfully enduring what life brings our way; (d) to give thanks to God for the glorious redemption he has provided for us through the blood of his Son, a redemption that has lifted us from darkness and enabled us to share in the inheritance of the saints.

The doctrinal section (1:15 - 2:23)

The pre-eminence of Christ (1:15 - 2:7). Paul here emphatically affirms the following truths about Christ:

1. Christ is the image of God (1:15). He is the perfect representation and manifestation of God.
2. Christ is the firstborn over all creation (1:15). This refers to precedence in rank rather than precedence in time. Put Christ alongside any created being, and he, the uncreated, has to be acknowledged as being supreme in authority and dignity.
3. Christ is the Creator (1:16). Instead of being created, Christ himself was the point of reference of creation. It was with a view to him that all things were created.

He is the point or goal to which all creation is tending.

4. Christ is the pre-existent one (1:17).
5. Christ is the preserver of all things (1:17).
6. Christ is the head of the church (1:18). By virtue of his resurrection, Christ is the beginning, the initiator, of the resurrection of his people. He is also the firstborn from the dead, that is, pre-eminent among his resurrected people.
7. Christ is the embodiment of all fulness (1:19). All there is of God resides in him.
8. Christ is the reconciler of all things (1:20-23). By receiving in his own body the wrath of God against sin (1 Peter 2:24), the Lord Jesus has removed the hostility between his people and God. Once God's enemies, they are now at peace with him.

Warning against error (2:8-23). In this section the apostle warns against false philosophy (2:8-15), legalism (2:16-17), angel worship (2:18-19) and asceticism (2:20-23).

The practical section (3:1 - 4:6)

Holiness in life (3:1-17). H. C. G. Moule calls the opening verses of this section 'one of the golden paragraphs of the whole Bible'.[2] In these verses the apostle lays out for us the root principle of the Christian life, that is, our union with Christ. The implications of this union can be laid out in terms of what has already taken place in the Christian and what will yet take place (3:1-4). These glorious realities place a demand upon the Christian to seek and to set his mind on heavenly things (3:1), to put aside sins (3:5-11) and to put on the love (3:12-14), the peace (3:15), the Word (3:16) and the name of Christ (3:17).

Holiness in the home (3:18 - 4:1). Paul's instructions for living in the home closely parallel those which he gave in his letter to the Ephesians (Eph. 5:22 - 6:9).

A request for prayer (4:2-4). Paul recognized that no minister of Christ ever progresses to the point when he is no longer in need of the prayers of God's people. Although Paul had spoken boldly and effectively in the past, he still urged the Colossians to pray fervently for him.

Concern for outsiders (4:5-6). Paul urges the Colossians to walk wisely and speak graciously. In so doing they will be 'redeeming the time', that is, making full use of their opportunities to influence those around them who did not know Christ.

Conclusion (4:7-18)

Paul closes by sharing personal notes about several brothers in Christ. This section abounds with warm-hearted affection and gratitude.

QUESTIONS FOR DISCUSSION

DISCUSS IT

1. Paul urged the Colossians to stand against false teachings. How can we resist the false teachings of our time? Read Acts 17:10-11; 1 John 4:1-6.

2. Paul told the Colossians to 'seek those things which are above' (3:1). What do the following passages teach us about seeking? Read 1 Chronicles 16:11; 22:19; Psalm 27:4,8; 63:1-8; Proverbs 2:1-4; Isaiah 55:6-7; Matthew 6:33.

CHAPTER
FORTY-THREE

THE FIRST AND SECOND EPISTLES OF PAUL TO THE THESSALONIANS

BIBLE BOOK

THE FIRST AND SECOND EPISTLES OF PAUL TO THE THESSALONIANS

1 THESSALONIANS

Introduction

INTRODUCTION

The Thessalonian letters were written by the apostle Paul to the church in the city of Thessalonica. This city, capital of the Roman province of Macedonia, was visited by Paul on his second missionary journey (Acts 17:1). His visit sparked off a riot!

Paul wrote his first letter to the Thessalonians in A.D. 51, after Timothy visited the church and reported back to the apostle on developments there.

Purpose

1 Thessalonians was written to express his gratitude for the progress of the believers there and to encourage them in their walk with the Lord. It was also written to clear up confusion that existed in the church about the return of the Lord.

Structure

Introduction (1:1)
1. Paul's thanksgiving (1:2-10)
2. Paul's testimony (2:1 - 3:13)
3. Paul's teaching (4:1 - 5:22)
Conclusion (5:23-28)

Overview

Introduction (1:1)

This greeting resembles those in Paul's other letters with one difference: Paul does not identify himself as an apostle.

Paul's thanksgiving (1:2-10)

Paul expresses thanks to the Lord for the faith, love and hope of the church (vv. 2-4). All of this was due to the gospel coming to them in power, in the Holy Spirit and with much assurance (v. 5). He was also grateful that the Thessalonians had become examples to other believers (vv. 6-10).

This section includes a wonderful summary of the true Christian:

1. He has turned from his idols (v. 9)
2. He serves the living and true God (v. 9)
3. He waits for the Lord to return from heaven (v. 10)

Paul's testimony (2:1 - 3:13)

In this section the apostle describes his ministry among the Thessalonians (2:1-12) and thanks God for their warm-hearted reception of him (2:13-16). He also explains how he came to send Timothy to them (2:17 - 3:5) and how he rejoiced over Timothy's report (3:6-10). Finally, he prays that he will soon be able to visit them.

This part of Paul's letter speaks powerfully to ministers about the conduct of their ministry. Paul had come to the Thessalonians with deep persuasion of the truth (2:2), with the goal of pleasing God rather than men (2:4), without flattering words and covetousness (2:5), and with the tenderness of a 'nursing mother' lovingly caring for her children (2:6-7).

The Thessalonians had warmly received Paul's ministry. They embraced his message, 'not as the word of men', but rather as the word of God (2:13).

We should also notice that this portion of Paul's letter contains valuable teaching on the matter of Christian suffering. Paul says that suffering should not startle us (2:18) or stop us from serving the Lord and trusting him (2:17; 3:1-8). It should, on the other hand, stimulate us to joyful appreciation (3:9) and to prayerful concern (3:10-13).

TEACHING

Paul's teaching (4:1 - 5:22)

On godly living (4:1-12). Paul calls upon the Thessalonians to follow the Lord's commandments (v. 2). He specifically urges them to be sexually pure (vv. 3-8), to love each other (v. 9) and to strive for a quiet and industrious life.

On the Lord's return (4:13 - 5:22). The Thessalonians evidently had some misconception about their believing loved ones who had died. Some apparently thought these would not finally be saved. Others seemed to think they would somehow be at some sort of disadvantage when the Lord returns. Paul urges his readers not to sorrow hopelessly (v. 13). He tells them that the dead in Christ will be raised first when Christ returns (4:13-16) and that living Christians will be caught up to meet the Lord in the air (4:17-18).

Paul also exhorts the Thessalonians not to sleep without due regard for the coming of the Lord. They are to heed the nature of Christ's coming (5:1-3), the nature of their calling (5:4-11), the needs of others (5:12-15) and the needs of their own hearts (5:16-18).

Conclusion (5:23-28)

Paul closes his letter with a prayer (v. 23), an assurance (v. 24), a request (v. 25), instructions (vv. 26-27) and a final wish (v. 28).

2 THESSALONIANS

Introduction

A few months after writing 1 Thessalonians, Paul added this letter. *The Open Bible* says: 'The bearer of the first epistle may have brought Paul an update on the new developments, prompting him to write this letter. They were still undergoing persecution, and the false teaching about the day of the Lord led some of them to over-react by giving up their jobs.'[1]

Purpose

Paul wrote, then, to encourage them regarding persecution, to correct their misconceptions about the return of the Lord and to exhort them to fulfil various duties.

Structure

Introduction (1:1-2)
1. Instructions (1:3 - 2:12)
   a. Regarding persecution (1:3-12)
   b. Regarding Christ's coming (2:1-12)
2. Thanksgiving (2:13-17)

TEACHING

3. Exhortations (3:1-15)
Conclusion (3:16-18)

Overview

The major themes of 2 Thessalonians are persecution, the Lord's return and the need for godly living.

Regarding the first of these, Paul reminds the Thessalonians that the Lord will bring judgement in his own time upon those who were persecuting them (1:5-10).

Regarding the Lord's return, Paul urges the Thessalonians not to be troubled by those who were suggesting that the second coming of Christ had already taken place. He clearly says this blessed event will not occur until two things have taken place: a great falling away from the faith, and the appearance of the man of sin, the Antichrist (2:3).

Regarding the need for godly living, Paul exhorts the Thessalonians not to give way to idleness, but rather to work hard (3:6-13).

QUESTIONS FOR DISCUSSION

1. Paul says 'the Lord himself' will return (1 Thess. 4:16). The same promise is given in the following passages:

DISCUSS IT

John 14:1-3; Acts 1:9-11. What does this promise mean to you?

2. *Read 1 Corinthians 15:35-58. What can we learn about the bodies believers will have when Christ raises them from the dead? Note 1 Corinthians 15:58. How should believers live in light of the glory that awaits them?*

THE GUIDE

CHAPTER
FORTY-FOUR

THE FIRST EPISTLE OF PAUL TO TIMOTHY

BIBLE BOOK

THE FIRST EPISTLE OF PAUL TO TIMOTHY

Introduction

Three of Paul's letters are known as the 'Pastoral Epistles' because they are concerned with the duties of those who are called to lead local churches. While Paul's previous letters were written to churches, these are written to individuals. They are Paul's last three letters, written near the end of his life.

Two of these letters went to Timothy and one to Titus. The first letter, 1 Timothy, was written around A.D. 63. Timothy was raised in a godly home (2 Tim. 1:5; 3:15), and came to know the Lord through Paul's ministry (1 Tim. 1:12). The apostle added him to his missionary team at Lystra and eventually sent him to pastor the church in Ephesus.

Purpose

Timothy was caught in what might be considered a devastating crossfire. On one hand, the times were extremely difficult and not at all hospitable towards the gospel (2 Tim. 3:1-9). On the other hand, Timothy was facing challenging problems in the church. Such things would have been difficult enough for the strongest of men, but Timothy was anything but strong. In addition to being prone to a spirit of fear and timidity (2 Tim. 1:6-8), he suffered from physical problems (1 Tim. 5:23). Things had become so bad in Ephesus that Timothy had evidently asked Paul to give him a new assignment.

Refusing Timothy's request (1 Tim. 1:3), Paul writes to give him careful instruction on how to deal with the problems in Ephesus. Paul also sprinkles in words of encouragement.

Structure

Introduction (1:1-2)
 1. A charge regarding false doctrine (1:3-20)
 2. Instructions regarding public worship (2:1 - 3:16)
    a. Prayer (2:1-8)
    b. Women (2:9-15)
    c. Leadership (3:1-13)
    d. Another charge (3:14-16)
 3. Instructions regarding the minister (4:1 - 6:19)
    a. Warning of apostasy (4:1-5)
    b. Various exhortations, including two additional charges (4:6 - 6:19)
       1. The minister's personal life (4:6-16)

2. The minister's relationship to others (5:1 - 6:10)

3. The minister and material wealth (6:11-19)

Conclusion — a closing charge (6:20-21)

Overview

Introduction (1:1-2)

Paul's opening words identify himself as an apostle of Christ and express his deep appreciation for Timothy as 'a true son in the faith' (v. 2).

A charge regarding false doctrine (1:3-20)

Paul quickly moves to one of the problems that was troubling Timothy and the church of Ephesus: false teachers. These teachers yearned to be known as great teachers of the law of Moses (v. 7). One of the ways to make a mark as a teacher is to find insights no one else has discovered. These teachers were evidently doing this in two ways. First, they were lifting names out of the genealogical lists of the Old Testament and spinning elaborate stories around them (v. 4). In other words, they were taking something that had a historical base and were building on it a huge superstructure of speculation. The same thing is often done in films on biblical episodes.

TEACHING

Secondly, these teachers were finding insights that went beyond the clear scope of the law of God. They were using the law of God in an unlawful way (v. 8). The lawful use of the law was to teach it as given by God to Israel, that is, to reveal God's standard of righteousness and their inability to live up to it, all of which was designed to drive them to faith in the coming Christ.

In other words, the law of God was designed to show us all that we are guilty of violating God's standards, and are, therefore, sentenced to eternal condemnation. To illustrate this, the apostle gives a list of things condemned by the law of God (vv. 9-10).

After warning Timothy about these false teachers, Paul proceeds to celebrate the power of the gospel of Christ. This gospel had created a great change in Paul (vv. 12-13) and had left him with utmost confidence in its reliability (v. 15) and with a heart full of praise (v. 17). This section closes with the first of Paul's charges (vv. 18-20).

Instructions regarding the church (2:1 - 3:16)

In this section Paul specifically deals with three matters: prayer (2:1-8), the role of women (2:9-15) and qualifications of pastors and deacons (3:1-13). The section ends with what may be considered to be another charge (3:14-16 — 'conduct yourself in the house of God').

It is clear from his discussion of these matters that Paul placed a high premium on public worship. His

discussion forces us to ask ourselves if we do the same.

On the matter of prayer, Paul stresses the following: its importance (2:1 — 'first of all' means 'as a matter of supreme priority'), its focus (2:1 — 'all men'), its motive (2:3) and its means (vv. 4-7 — on the basis of the finished work of Christ).

On the matter of women in worship, Paul calls for modest dress (2:9-10), good works (2:10) and an understanding of God's created order (2:11-15).

On the matter of leadership, Paul lists qualifications for both pastors (3:1-7) and deacons (3:8-13).

Instructions regarding the minister (4:1 - 6:19)

Paul devotes the last half of his letter to describing for Timothy the type of minister he should aspire to be. This section includes two additional charges (4:11-16; 5:21-25).

Paul begins this portion of his letter by sharing with Timothy a revelation that he had received from the Holy Spirit, namely, that they were about to embark upon a time of falling away from the faith. This would be created by false teachers paying heed to 'deceiving spirits' (4:1) and subsequently teaching false doctrine. These teachers would offer a brand of spirituality through severe treatment of the body (4:3).

TEACHING

Having warned Timothy of this threat to the faith, Paul calls upon his son in the ministry to give earnest heed to himself as a minister of the gospel. He is to earn respect by being a good example (4:12), to practise a biblical ministry (4:13), to develop his God-given ability (4:14), to be totally absorbed in his work (4:15) and to be continually and diligently careful about his life and doctrine (4:16).

This is followed by instructions on relating to various groups in the church, especially widows (5:3-16) and elders (5:17-20).

Yet another area of concern for the minister is the matter of handling material wealth. Paul called upon Timothy to flee from the love of money (6:6-11) and to command the rich not to trust in their wealth but rather in the living God (6:17) and to use their wealth to do good works (6:18-19). It was essential for Timothy to realize that true riches are found in living for God. Timothy must, therefore, pursue spiritual qualities (6:11), fight the good fight of faith (6:12), lay hold of eternal life (6:12), and keep 'the commandment' (6:13-16,20), which may be a reference to the entire Word of God.

Conclusion — a closing charge (6:20-21)

Paul closes with a final charge. Timothy is to view the gospel as a valuable treasure that has been entrusted to him and is to guard it diligently and faithfully.

DISCUSS IT

1. Paul stresses public worship in 1 Timothy. Read Psalms 84 and 100. What do these psalms teach us about worship?

2. How are the people of God to treat true ministers? Read 1 Corinthians 9:1-18; Ephesians 6:18-20; 1 Thessalonians 5:12-13; Hebrews 13:17.

THE GUIDE

CHAPTER
FORTY-FIVE

THE SECOND EPISTLE OF PAUL TO TIMOTHY

2 TIMOTHY

BIBLE BOOK

THE SECOND EPISTLE OF PAUL TO TIMOTHY

Introduction

INTRODUCTION

2 Timothy is the last of Paul's letters. It was evidently written towards the end of his second Roman imprisonment and shortly before his death (4:6). It is generally thought that Paul was beheaded during the emperor Nero's persecution of Christians. Since Nero himself was killed in A.D. 68, a date of A.D. 66 or 67 would seem to be correct for Paul's writing of 2 Timothy.

Purpose

Paul's purpose in writing was twofold. First, he wanted Timothy to come from Ephesus and visit him in Rome as quickly as possible (4:9,21). Secondly, he wanted to encourage Timothy to be a faithful minister of the Lord Jesus Christ (1:13; 2:15; 3:14; 4:5).

Structure

Introduction (1:1-2)
1. Thanksgiving (1:3-7)
2. A call to endure (1:8-18)
   a. In the face of sufferings (1:8-12)
   b. In the face of desertions (1:13-18)
3. A call to teach (2:1-26)
4. A call to understand (3:1-17)
5. A call to preach (4:1-8)
Conclusion (4:9-22)

Overview

Introduction (1:1-2)

Paul identifies himself as an apostle of Christ and addresses Timothy as 'a beloved son'. Paul was referring, of course, to Timothy as a son in the ministry.

Thanksgiving (1:3-7)

The apostle fervently thanked the Lord for the faith of Timothy, as well as that of his grandmother and mother. He also assured Timothy of his prayers and, knowing Timothy's inclination to be timid and fearful, urged him to stir up his gift. There was no need for Timothy to give in to a cowardly fear because the Lord has given the necessary power, love and discipline to faithfully serve him.

A call to endure (1:8-18)

In this section Paul moves to the main theme of his letter: endurance. The word 'endure' appears in verses 2:3,10 and 12. Paul also urges Timothy to 'hold fast' (1:13) and to 'continue' (3:14).

Faithful endurance in the ministry was no small task. Paul, the leading spokesman of Christianity, was writing from prison. Many, intimidated and cowered by Paul's imprisonment, had already turned from him. Especially painful to Paul were the defections of Phygellus and Hermogenes (1:15) and Demas (4:10).

Not all, of course, had forsaken Paul. Onesiphorous stood out as a shining beacon of devotedness (1:16-18). Paul wanted Timothy to follow the example of this man, to be unashamed about the apostle's imprisonment even as he had been (1:16). This was a very important matter. Paul was in prison for his 'testimony' to the Lord (1:8). To be ashamed of Paul's imprisonment was, then, the same as being ashamed of the gospel that led to it.

Our willingness to stand for the gospel will be in direct proportion to our understanding of it. Paul reminds Timothy of the essential core of the gospel (1:9-10) and assures him that he, Paul, had not wavered in embracing it. Paul was not only unashamed of his own imprisonment (1:12) but was resting completely upon his Lord (1:12).

A call to teach (2:1-26)

Paul called Timothy to an active endurance. Timothy was not just to hold tenaciously to the gospel within his own mind and heart, he was to actively share it with others. He was to commit specifically to faithful men what he had learned from Paul (2:2).

To be effective in this endeavour Timothy would have to keep in mind the following examples or patterns:

1. *the soldier* (2:3-4). The soldier has to be willing to endure hardship and to disentangle himself from civilian affairs.
2. *the athlete* (2:5). The athlete cannot win if he breaks the rules. The minister of the gospel must put into practice what he teaches.
3. *the farmer* (2:6). As the farmer cannot expect a good crop apart from constant toil, so the minister cannot expect a spiritual crop without putting forth persistent, dedicated labour.

The task of being a good teacher also required Timothy to:

1. study diligently (2:15)
2. shun the empty and vain speculation of false teachers (2:16-18)
3. strive to be a clean and useful vessel (2:19-21)
4. flee youthful lusts (2:22)
5. be gentle, patient and humble (2:24-26)

TEACHING

A call to understand (3:1-17)

Timothy could not conduct an effective ministry without understanding 'the last days'. These days began with the first coming of Christ (Acts 2:14-17; Heb. 1:1-2) and will continue until his second coming. Paul lists several characteristics of these days. In summary we may say they are characterized by a moral degeneracy and a religious perversity that will increase and intensify (3:13) as this period draws to an end.

Lest Timothy be overwhelmed with this description of the last days, Paul quickly proceeds to assure him that he has in Scripture a sufficient resource for withstanding evil (3:15-17). The fact that Scripture is the product of divine inspiration assures us that it is sufficient for:

1. doctrine — God's truth about himself and about us
2. reproof — refuting error and false teachings
3. correction — straightening believers in their spirit and practice
4. instruction in righteousness — providing guidance in every area of duty

A call to preach (4:1-8)

Such a perfect and powerful resource as Scripture requires proclamation. The apostle calls

Timothy to this task in these well-known words: 'Preach the word!' (4:2).

This preaching is to be undertaken 'in season and out of season' (4:2). Timothy is to both take and make opportunities for preaching. It is to consist of an intellectual dimension ('convince'), a moral dimension ('rebuke') and an emotional dimension ('exhort'). It is to be carried out in the face of all kinds of false teachers and amidst a climate of willingness to embrace the sensational and novel (4:3-4).

Paul himself had demonstrated the type of ministry Timothy was to exercise, and now Paul had reached the end. He was able to say that he had fought a good fight, finished his race and kept the faith, and he was looking forward to his reward (4:6-8). Every minister should aspire to be able to say the same at the end of his ministry.

Conclusion (4:9-22)

Paul's closing words cover a wide array of individuals, some of whom had done him much harm. The apostle's testimony was that the Lord had strengthened him in the midst of evil (4:17) and that the same Lord was about to deliver him from it completely (4:18). Paul could not help but praise such a faithful and gracious Lord: 'To him be glory for ever and ever. Amen!' (4:18).

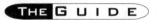

DISCUSS IT

1. One of the apostle's admonitions to Timothy was 'hold fast' (1:13). Look at the following verses: 1 Thessalonians 5:21; Titus 1:9; Hebrews 3:6; 4:14; Revelation 2:25; 3:11. What do they teach us regarding 'holding fast'?

2. Read Acts 2:14-17; Hebrews 1:1-2. When are the last days?

THE GUIDE

THE EPISTLES OF PAUL TO TITUS AND PHILEMON

THE EPISTLES OF PAUL TO TITUS AND PHILEMON

TITUS

Introduction

This letter was written by the apostle Paul, in approximately A.D. 63, to the young minister whose name it bears. Titus, a Greek, was one of Paul's converts. He had accompanied Paul on some of his travels, had himself answered God's call to the ministry and had been left by Paul to minister on the island of Crete.

Titus' ministry there was, like Timothy's in Ephesus, very slow and discouraging. It appears that he was facing a twofold dilemma. Firstly, the false teachers who posed such a threat to other churches were also found in Crete. Secondly, the church members were lacking in good works. They evidently thought it was possible to have a true and genuine faith without it affecting their lives.

Purpose

Paul's purpose in writing to Titus was to issue a clear call to sound doctrine and good works. The

word 'sound' appears five times in this short letter
(1:9,13; 2:1,2,8). The words 'good works' appear six
times (1:16; 2:7,14; 3:1,8,14).

Structure

Introduction (1:1-4)
1. Appoint elders (1:5-9)
2. Rebuke false teachers (1:10-16)
3. Instruct believers (2:1 - 3:11)
   a. Of the duties of particular age groups (2:2 - 3:2)
   b. Of the incentives for godly living (3:3-11)
Conclusion (3:12-15)

Overview

Introduction (1:1-4)

In this lengthy introduction (only Galatians and
Romans contain one which is longer), Paul first identifies himself (vv. 1-3) and greets Titus (1:4).

Appoint elders (1:5-9)

When Paul left Titus in Crete he instructed him to 'set
in order the things that are lacking, and appoint elders
in every city' (1:5). We have noted the things that were
lacking, namely, sound doctrine and good works. These
deficiencies were obviously too great for Titus to address by himself, hence the need for godly elders. The

fact that Paul now reminds Titus of this command should not be taken to mean that Titus had forgotten it. It should rather be understood as the apostle underscoring the urgency of it.

Rebuke false teachers (1:10-16)

These teachers were from the section of 'Judaizers' that insisted that one could not be saved by faith in Christ alone but rather by faith in Christ plus the keeping of the law of Moses. To their way of thinking, the Jewish rituals and regulations made them pure in the eyes of God. Paul responds by saying that all things are pure to those who have been made pure by faith.

Instruct believers (2:1 - 3:11)

The second chapter of Titus begins with a strong contrast: 'But as for you...' Those words make it clear that Titus was to be totally different from the false teachers. In addition to teaching sound doctrine, he was to teach the kind of life that corresponds to it. In particular, Titus was to give the men and women of various ages and stations in life instruction in godliness, warning them of the dangers and calling them to the responsibilities that pertained to their age group or station.

With the word 'for' (3:3), the apostle calls Titus away from instructions to the various ages to the incentives for such instructions. The grace of God is the motivating power for the ethical demands placed on the Christian. Paul celebrates that grace in this portion of his letter (3:3-8) as well as in his earlier words about the conduct of servants (2:11-14). The following aspects of that grace are apparent in these portions:

1. *our need for God's grace* (3:3). This verse gives us what Geoffrey Wilson refers to as 'a mournful proof of the depravity of human nature'.[1]

2. *the channel of God's grace* (2:11; 3:4). God's grace was manifested ('appeared') in the coming of Christ to this earth to provide eternal salvation for sinners. How did Christ do this? It was by 'giving himself for us', that is, by taking the place of sinners and receiving their condemnation on the cross.

3. *the operations of God's grace* (3:5,7). Salvation may be likened to a 'washing' (3:5) which consists of regeneration and renewal. The former consists of God planting new life within. The latter consists of the Holy Spirit delivering from sin and renewing the image of God within. Paul also uses the word 'justified' (3:7) to describe the salvation we have through Christ. It is that act of God whereby he counts the believer's sins to be Christ's and Christ's righteousness to be the believer's.

Because of these matchless benefits, Christians have a 'blessed hope' (2:13).

4. *the demands of God's grace* (2:12; 3:8). The grace that saves from eternal condemnation demands that we show our gratitude for this deliverance by living 'soberly, righteously, and godly in the present age' (2:12).

Conclusion (3:12-15)

Paul concludes his letter with some personal notes and with a final plea for Titus to urge his congregation to 'maintain good works' (3:14).

PHILEMON

This very brief letter constitutes Paul's most personal and private correspondence. It was written by the apostle, during his first Roman imprisonment, to Philemon, a Christian in Colosse. The date of the letter is A.D. 62.

Paul wrote to Philemon regarding the latter's slave, Onesimus. Onesimus had robbed his master Philemon (vv. 10,11,16,18) and then fled to Rome. There he happened to encounter the apostle Paul who led him to the Lord. Paul then sent Onesimus, accompanied by Tychichus and this letter, back to Philemon (vv. 12,15,16). He urged Philemon to receive Onesimus 'no longer as a slave but more than a slave, as a beloved brother' (v. 16).

Paul also assured Philemon that he, Paul, was willing to pay for any damages caused by

Onesimus. This letter, consisting of only 355 Greek words, has been credited with putting into place the principles that eventually caused the end of slavery.

On this matter, the *MacArthur Study Bible* observes: 'The NT nowhere directly attacks slavery; had it done so, the resulting slave insurrections would have been brutally suppressed and the message of the gospel hopelessly confused with that of social reform. Instead, Christianity undermined the evils of slavery by changing the hearts of slaves and masters. By stressing the spiritual equality of master and slave (v. 16; Gal. 3:28; Eph. 6:9; Col. 4:1; 1 Tim. 6:1,2), the Bible did away with slavery's abuses.'[2]

The letter consists of an introduction (vv. 1-7), the appeal (vv. 8-21), and a conclusion (vv. 22-25).

It speaks to us about the power of Christ to forgive sinners and the resulting demand for Christ's people to practise forgiveness towards one another.

QUESTIONS FOR DISCUSSION

1. Study the following verses: Matthew 7:21-23; Romans 4:1-25; Ephesians 2:10. Can good works save us? Will those who are saved manifest it in good works?

2. Titus calls the Christian's hope 'blessed' (2:13). Read 2 Thessalonians 2:16; Hebrews 6:19; 7:19; 1 Peter 1:3. What words do these verses use to describe the believer's hope?

THE GUIDE

CHAPTER
FORTY-SEVEN

THE EPISTLE TO
THE HEBREWS

BIBLE BOOK

THE EPISTLE TO THE HEBREWS

Introduction

There is no consensus on the identity of the author of Hebrews. Many think it was the apostle Paul, but Barnabas, Timothy and Apollos have also been suggested.

There is also uncertainty about the recipients of this letter. They were obviously Jews who had professed faith in Christ, but their location is unknown. Jerusalem, Greece, Rome and Alexandria have all been mentioned as possibilities, but we cannot identify these Jews with certainty.

The fact that the destruction of Jerusalem in A.D. 70 is not mentioned indicates that it was written before then, perhaps between A.D. 64 and 68.

Purpose

One thing that is clear about this letter is its purpose. These professing Christians were showing signs of drifting back to their former religion of Judaism. They had made a good beginning, but the combined pressures of persecution and false teaching were causing them to lose heart. This author wrote to arrest their drift (2:1) and encourage them in their faith. He sought to do this by emphasizing both the superiority of Christ and the necessity of faith.

Structure

1. The superiority of Christ (1:1 - 10:39)
   a. Superior to the prophets (1:1-3)
   b. Superior to the angels (1:4 - 2:18)
   c. First exhortation (2:1-4)
   d. Superior despite humiliation (2:5-18)
   e. Superior to Moses (3:1-6)
   f. Second exhortation (3:7 - 4:13)
   g. Superior in his priesthood (4:14 - 10:18); Third exhortation (5:11 - 6:20)
   h. Fourth exhortation (10:19-39)
2. The necessity of faith (11:1 - 13:17)
   a. Examples of faith (11:1-40)
   b. The endurance of faith (12:1-11)
   c. Fifth exhortation (12:12-29)
   d. The evidences of faith (13:1-17)

Conclusion (13:18-25)

Overview

The superiority of Christ (1:1 - 10:39)

The author seeks to arrest his readers' drift back to Judaism by placing its most venerated people and objects alongside the Lord Jesus Christ. As he does so, these persons and objects, no matter how exalted and venerated by the Jewish mind, pale in comparison.

Superior to the prophets (1:1-3). Christ is superior to the prophets in both his message and his person. Their message was partial. It came at various times and in various ways. The message of Christ, on the other hand, is final in terms of time (nothing more to come) and content (nothing more to be said).

The Lord Jesus is superior in his person because he is the heir of all things, God's creative agent, the brightness of God's glory, God's express image, God's cosmic sustainer and God's perfect sacrifice.

Superior to the angels (1:4-14). Christ is superior to the angels because he is the eternal Son of God (1:5) and all the angels have been commanded to worship him (1:6). The angels, on the other hand, are not equal to God but rather are 'sent forth to minister for those who will inherit salvation' (1:14).

First exhortation (2:1-4). These verses bring us to the first of the author's five exhortations. He urges his readers to 'give the more earnest heed' to the message they had received so that they do not drift away. Their earnest attention was necessary because of the certainty of the truth of the gospel message and the greatness of the salvation it conveys.

Superior despite humiliation (2:5-18). The author here anticipates an objection: How can superiority be claimed for Christ in light of the fact that he was a man and died as all men do? The author responds by insisting that the humiliation of Christ in no way eroded his superiority, but was necessary for our eternal salvation.

Superior to Moses (3:1-6). The Jews greatly revered Moses, but Christ was superior to him as the builder of a house is superior to the house. Furthermore, while Moses was a servant, Christ is the Son.

Second exhortation (3:7 - 4:13). The readers are exhorted not to repeat the error of the Israelites under Moses who failed to enter the land of Canaan because of their unbelief.

Superior in his priesthood (4:14 - 10:18); Third exhortation (5:11 - 6:20). Christ is superior in his priesthood because he is from a better order, the order of Melchizedek, which represents permanence (7:1-28); he mediates a better covenant (8:1-13); he conducts his priesthood in a superior place, the heavenly sanctuary (9:1-15); and he conducts it on a superior basis, that is, the sacrifice of himself once and for all (9:16 - 10:18).

This section includes the third exhortation (5:11 - 6:20) in which the author warns his readers about being 'dull of hearing' (5:11).

Fourth exhortation (10:19-39). Here the author issues a warning that to turn back from a profession of faith would lead to fearful judgement. (Note: the warning passages in Hebrews 6:4-8 and 10:19-39 do not teach that a true child of God can lose his salvation. They warn rather about the danger of professing faith without possessing it.)

The necessity of faith (11:1 - 13:17)

Examples of faith (11:1-40). The author encourages his readers to remain faithful by reminding them of the men and women of the Old Testament who remained true to the Lord in spite of facing enormous difficulties and challenges.

The endurance of faith (12:1-11). The Lord Jesus Christ himself is, of course, the supreme example of endurance. The Hebrew Christians could find strength to endure by looking to the Lord, who did not allow anything to deter him from the cross (12:2-3). The author also includes in this section a warning about chastisement for children of God who were not 'striving against sin' (12:4).

Fifth exhortation (12:12-29). The final exhortation calls the readers to spiritual vitality by strengthening and straightening themselves in the things of the Lord.

The evidences of faith (13:1-17). Our faithfulness to the Lord is demonstrated in practical ways. It results in compassion for those in need (vv. 1-3) and in contentment (vv. 4-5). It is also expressed in thanksgiving to the Lord (v. 15), in deeds of kindness (v. 16) and in submissiveness to spiritual leaders (v. 17).

Conclusion (13:18-25)

The author closes his letter by requesting prayer for himself (vv. 18-19), by pronouncing a wonderful benediction upon his readers (vv. 20-21), by appealing to them to heed what he had written (v. 22) and by adding a few personal notes (vv. 23-25).

QUESTIONS FOR DISCUSSION

1. 'Apostasy' is a falling away from the truth of God. Who are some well-known apostates in Scripture?

2. The author of Hebrews warns about the possibility of chastisement (12:3-11). Read David's description of his chastisement in Psalm 32. Was God's chastisement severe? What did it produce?

THE GUIDE

CHAPTER
FORTY-EIGHT

THE EPISTLE OF JAMES

JAMES

THE EPISTLE OF JAMES

INTRODUCTION

Introduction

There can be little doubt that this book was written by James, the half-brother of Jesus. (230 words of this letter closely resemble the words of James in his message at the Jerusalem Council — Acts 15:13-21.) The book of James is considered to be the earliest of all the New Testament epistles. It was probably written some time between A.D. 45 and 50.

Purpose

James wrote to Jewish Christians who were 'scattered abroad'. The book of Acts tells us the Christians in Jerusalem were compelled by persecution to scatter throughout Judea and Samaria (Acts 8:1) and even as far as Phoenicia, Cyprus and Antioch (Acts 11:19). Fleeing did not always solve the problem as many Christians also encountered persecution in their new homes.

The trials of life often shake our faith and cause us to lessen our service. In other words, hardships and difficulties can diminish the reality of religion. James wrote to help his readers experience such reality.

Structure

Greeting (1:1)
1. The pressures that diminish reality in religion (1:2-17)
2. The power that delivers reality in religion (1:18-25)
3. The practices that demonstrate reality in religion (1:26 - 5:6)
   a. Stated (1:26-27)
   b. Elaborated (2:1 - 5:6)
Conclusion (5:7-20)

Distinguishing features

1. This letter is filled with imperatives (54 occurrences in 108 verses), which indicates that James was speaking with authority.
2. The style is engaging. James used numerous examples and comparisons taken from nature and human life.
3. The letter includes numerous references to Old Testament history: Abraham, Isaac, Rahab, Job and Elijah are mentioned. This constitutes additional

evidence that James wrote to a Jewish readership.

4. James echoes much of what Jesus said in the Sermon on the Mount. Compare the following verses from Matthew with verses from James.

Matthew	James
7:7	1:5
7:11	1:17
7:24	1:22
5:3	2:5
7:12	2:8
5:7	2:13
7:16	3:12
5:9	3:18
7:1	4:11
6:19	5:2

Overview

Greeting (1:1)

The pressures that diminish reality in religion (1:2-17)

James draws a distinction between trials (vv. 2-12) and temptations (vv. 13-17). God sends trials to his people to produce patience (v. 3), but the Lord never tempts anyone to sin (v. 13). Satan uses our own sinful desires to entice us to sin (v. 14). The Lord, on the other hand, is the source of all good gifts (v. 17). The distinction between trials and temptations may be put in this way: God sends trials to bring out the best in us; Satan sends temptations to bring out the worst in us.

The power that delivers reality in religion (1:18-25)

The Christian has in the Word of God the resource he needs for enduring trials and temptations. The power of that Word was decisively demonstrated in his own conversion. Each Christian has been saved by the grace of God working in and through the Word of God (1:18).

The power that worked so mightily in conversion is available for Christian living. It must, however, be appropriated. How do we appropriate the power of the Word of God? We must hear (vv. 19-20), receive (v. 21) and obey it (vv. 22-25).

The practices that demonstrate reality in religion (1:26 - 5:6)

With these things in place, James moves to the heart of his letter. He first states three marks of reality in religion (1:26-27) and then devotes the major part of his letter to elaborating upon them (2:1 - 5:6). The marks are as follows:

1. control of the tongue (1:26)
2. care for the needy (1:27)
3. separation from the world (1:27)

James does not discuss these marks in the same order in which he stated them. He begins with the second, caring for the needy (2:1-26), moves to controlling the tongue (3:1-12) and closes with maintaining separation from the world (3:13 - 5:6).

Caring for the needy (2:1-26). In this section James warns his readers to be on guard against two attitudes that destroy a caring ministry: the attitude of partiality (vv. 1-13) and the attitude that one can have faith without works (vv. 14-26).

The second of these brings us to the central question about James' letter, namely, whether he intended to contradict Paul's teaching that salvation is by the grace of God and not due at all to our works. Many, on the basis of what James says in 2:14, have concluded as much. But this verse shows quite the opposite. James does not say 'if someone has faith' but rather 'if someone says he has faith'. James was dealing with those who professed faith in Christ but showed no evidence of it. Paul himself insisted that genuine faith leads to good works (Eph. 2:10). True faith always produces good works and good works are evidence of true faith.

TEACHING

Controlling the tongue (3:1-12). James elaborates on this mark of true religion by calling attention to the vital significance of controlling the tongue (vv. 1-2) and the enormous difficulty of doing so (vv. 3-12). Regarding the latter, he suggests that the tongue is small but extremely powerful (vv. 3-5); it is capable of great destruction (v. 6); it is untameable (vv. 7-8); and it is inconsistent (vv. 9-12).

Maintaining separation from the world (3:13 - 5:6). This mark requires that we drink from the right fountain, the fountain of wisdom (3:13-18), and that we discern our true foe, ourselves (4:1 - 5:6). Selfish living takes a toll on our relationship with others (4:1-2) as well as on our relationship with God (4:3-4). We can avoid it only if we submit to God (4:7), resist the devil (4:7), draw near to God (4:8), repent (4:8) and humble ourselves before God (4:10). We must also be on our guard against the special tendencies of self to defame others (4:11-12) and to govern our lives presumptuously (4:13-17).

Conclusion (5:7-20)

James closes his letter by appealing to his readers to do three things:

1. be patient (vv. 7-12)
2. pray (vv. 13-18)
3. restore those who stray (vv. 19-20)

DISCUSS IT

The section on prayer includes a controversial section on the healing of the sick (vv. 14-16). The anointing with oil may very well refer to medical treatment. The prayer of faith is not a prayer we work up. When it is God's will to heal, he gives the assurance to pray this prayer.

QUESTIONS FOR DISCUSSION

1. *How is the Christian to use his tongue? Read Ephesians 4:29-32; Philippians 1:27; Colossians 4:6; 1 Peter 2:12; 3:15.*

2. *Read the following passages — Psalm 25:9; Isaiah 57:15; 66:2; Matthew 11:28-30; Ephesians 4:1-3; Philippians 2:1-11; Colossians 3:12. What is the grace for which these verses call? Who is our example in developing this grace?*

CHAPTER
FORTY-NINE

THE FIRST
EPISTLE OF
PETER

1 PETER

BIBLE BOOK

THE FIRST EPISTLE OF PETER

Introduction

INTRODUCTION

The apostle Peter wrote this small letter to Christians who were scattered throughout five provinces in Asia Minor (1:1). These people were suffering severe persecution for their faith.

A large number of Bible scholars believe that Peter wrote this letter in A.D. 65 after the Roman emperor Nero began a widespread persecution of Christians in A.D. 64.

Purpose

The apostle wrote this letter to encourage his readers by reminding them of the sufficiency of God's grace. The word 'grace' is found in verses 1:2,10,13; 3:7; 4:10; 5:10,12.

Structure

Introduction (1:1-2)
1. Grace for salvation (1:3 - 2:12)

Overview

Introduction (1:1-2)

The apostle opens his letter by identifying himself as an apostle (v. 1), by identifying his readers (vv. 1-2), and by wishing for them grace and peace (v. 2).

Peter's introductory remarks should not be dismissed as a mere formality. Here he begins to celebrate the greatness of salvation, a topic that he will soon enlarge upon. He knew nothing could help his suffering readers more than to realize that their sufferings were temporary. Because of their great salvation they could look beyond this world to eternal glory.

What made their salvation great? It was planned and provided by the triune God. His readers were 'elect according to the foreknowledge of God' (v. 1). That means they were chosen by God before the world began. We have acute difficulty in reconciling God's choice of us with human responsibility, but the Bible insists both are true. We would do well to remember that Peter mentioned this truth, not to introduce a theological puzzle, but rather to assure his readers.

Peter also refers to the 'sanctification of the Spirit' and the 'sprinkling of the blood of Jesus Christ' (v. 2).

God had also chosen a distinct way for them to become his people, that is, through the Holy Spirit convicting them of their sins and through the atoning death of Jesus being applied to their hearts. No one becomes a child of God apart from these.

Grace for salvation (1:3 - 2:12)

In these verses the apostle explores in even more detail the greatness of salvation. It is great because it bestows rich benefits: a living hope (1:3), a lasting inheritance (1:4-5) and a joyful spirit (1:6-9). The second of these, the inheritance, is lasting because God both keeps it for us (1:4) and us for it (1:5).

Salvation is also great because it fulfilled prophecy (1:10-12). Regarding the Old Testament prophets, Peter stresses the following:

1. the source of their prophecies — the Holy Spirit (1:11)
2. the focus of their prophecies — the sufferings of Christ and the glories to follow (1:11)
3. the purpose of their prophecies — 'not to themselves, but to us' (1:12)
4. their response to their prophecies — 'inquired and searched carefully' (1:10)

Having established the greatness of salvation, Peter turns his attention to the appropriate response of the Christian. He shows what this response consists of (1:13-2:2) and how his readers could give this response, namely, by remembering who God is (1:16-17), who Christ is and what he has done (1:19-20), and who they themselves were through Christ. Concerning the latter, the apostle says they were called to be God's obedient children (1:14-15), redeemed from an unprofitable way of life (1:18), living stones (2:5), a holy and royal priesthood (2:5), a chosen generation (2:9), a holy nation (2:9), his own special people (2:9), the people of God (2:10) and recipients of mercy (2:10).

Grace for submission (2:13 - 3:12)

The apostle calls for submission in four vital areas:

1. *government* (2:13-17). The Christian is to recognize that government was given by God to punish evil and to reward good, and he is to freely submit to it except when it requires him to disobey God (Acts 4:19-20).

2. *secular employment* (2:18-19). The apostles did not condone slavery. They knew that as the gospel changed human hearts this institution would be eliminated. As long as slavery existed, Christian slaves were to use it to promote the gospel by doing their work willingly.

3. *marriage* (3:1-7). Many women were converted after they were married and were faced with the question of how to win their unbelieving husbands to the Lord. Peter calls them to do this by showing the beauty of a

life changed by Christ. He seems to assume that husbands would be living with believing wives, and he calls for them to highly honour and esteem their wives, recognizing that their wives are equal with them before God.

4. *church* (3:8-9). The church is to be a living demonstration of the difference Christianity makes, and it cannot achieve this if it is filled with discord.

Grace for suffering (3:13 - 4:19)

In this section Peter gives instructions for coping with suffering. He urges his readers to prevent suffering by living good lives (3:13), to make sure they were suffering for the right reason, that is, for righteousness' sake (3:14), and in the right way: without fear and stress (3:14), in dependence on God (3:15), with a readiness to explain their hope (3:15), with a good conscience (3:16), without being surprised (4:12) and with joy (4:13).

Grace for service (5:1-11)

It is interesting that Peter moves directly from his discussion of suffering to the fellowship of the church. He evidently wanted to tie the two things firmly together. The fellowship of the church ought to be a refuge for each child of God, a place where he or she finds strength to go out and face the world. Pastors and members must fulfil their responsibilities if the church is to be strong. Pastors must be willing shepherds (vv. 1-2) and worthy examples (vv. 3-4). Members must show humility towards each other (v. 5), cast their cares upon the Lord (v. 7) and resist Satan (vv. 8-9).

Conclusion (5:12-14)

Peter closes his epistle by giving a word of explanation for his writing (v. 12), by sharing a greeting from their brothers and sisters in Christ in Babylon (his way of designating Rome) and from Mark (v. 12). He further calls upon them to greet each other warmly (v. 14) and expresses his desire for them to enjoy peace (v. 14).

QUESTIONS FOR DISCUSSION

1. *Peter refers to his readers as 'elect according to the foreknowledge of God' (1:2). Where does God's election of his people lead? Read Romans 8:29; 9:23; Ephesians 1:5; 2:10; 2 Thessalonians 2:13.*

2. *Pastors are under-shepherds of the flock, serving under the Lord Jesus Christ, the Chief Shepherd (5:4). Read Isaiah 40:10-11. How does the Lord Jesus go about his shepherdly work? For a description of false shepherds, read Isaiah 56:11; Jeremiah 50:6; Ezekiel 34:1-10; and John 10:12-13.*

CHAPTER FIFTY

THE SECOND EPISTLE OF PETER AND THE EPISTLE OF JUDE

BIBLE BOOK

THE SECOND EPISTLE OF PETER AND THE EPISTLE OF JUDE

2 PETER

Introduction and purpose

The apostle Peter wrote his first epistle to Christians who were facing the danger of persecution. He wrote his second letter to the same Christians (3:1) about yet another very serious danger, that of false teachers. Satan always fishes with more than one hook.

Peter apparently wrote this letter shortly before his death (1:14), which is generally placed between A.D. 64 and 66.

Structure

Introduction (1:1-2)
1. A call to grow in grace (1:3-21)
2. A warning about false teachers (2:1-22)
3. A special area of concern (3:1-16)
A closing appeal (3:17-18)

Overview

Introduction (1:1-2)

Peter identifies himself as a servant and apostle of Christ and addresses his readers as those who shared his 'precious faith' (v. 1). He wishes them to enjoy grace and peace (v. 2), and then immediately flows into his emphasis on growth in grace. There is, then, no clear line of demarcation between Peter's introduction and the body of his letter.

A call to grow in grace (1:3-21)

It is interesting that Peter does not immediately begin to describe and warn against the false teachers about whom he was so concerned. Instead he does two things. Firstly, he urges his readers to grow as Christians. He knew the false teachers would have little effect on believers who were strong and robust in their faith and godly in their lives. Secondly, he reminds his readers that the message they had received, the very message the false teachers were challenging, was indisputably true.

The growth for which the apostle calls comes through trusting the God who has mighty power and who has given precious promises (vv. 3-4). It also comes about through the diligent effort of believers to flesh out their faith (vv. 5-11).

Furthermore, this growth comes about by remembering the trustworthiness of the message his readers had received. The false teachers were alleging that the apostles had delivered a defective message to the churches, that they had used 'cunningly devised fables' in preaching that Jesus was truly God in human flesh.

Peter emphatically denies this assertion. He points his readers to the experience that he and other disciples had on the Mount of Transfiguration. There they saw Jesus 'transfigured' before them. In other words, he showed himself to be God before their eyes. And they also heard God speak from heaven to own Jesus as his Son. But Peter offered even stronger evidence to support the trustworthiness of the apostles' message, that is, it fulfilled the prophecies of the Old Testament. What the apostles had seen in Christ perfectly matched what the prophets had predicted.

A warning about false teachers (2:1-22)

Here the apostle begins to deal with the false teachers themselves. He gives a general statement (vv. 1-3), a detailed description (vv. 10-18) and a solemn warning (vv. 19-22).

In the general statement, he affirms:

1. the inevitability of false teachers in the life of the church (v. 1)

2. the subtlety of such teachers — 'secretly bring in' (v. 1)
3. the nature of their teachings — 'destructive' (v. 1)
4. the enormity of their sin — Some think the phrase 'denying the Lord who bought them' refers to them rejecting the atonement Jesus made for them on the cross, but the Greek word translated 'Lord' (*despotes*) is never used for Jesus. It is, however, used for God the Father. Peter was probably saying these teachers were denying the God who had blessed them in various ways.
5. their terrible end — 'swift destruction' (v. 1)

In his detailed description, Peter says these teachers have no respect for authority (vv. 10-12) or morality (vv. 10,12-14). They were also greedy for gain (vv. 15-16) and failed to deliver what they had promised (vv. 17-18).

This chapter closes with Peter using the false teachers as a warning to his readers about the possibility of going a long way in religion without truly being saved (vv. 20-22).

A special area of concern (3:1-16); and a closing appeal (3:17-18)

In this chapter the apostle turns his attention to the area in which the false teachers seem to have focused their attack — the doctrine of Christ's return. He informs his readers of the arguments of the scoffers (vv. 3-4) and their folly (vv. 5-9). He then assures his readers

that the Lord will indeed come (v. 10) and urges
them to be ready (vv. 11-15).

JUDE

Introduction and purpose

The epistle of Jude was written by Jude, one of
the half-brothers of Jesus (Matt. 13:55), to some
Christians who were struggling with the same
problem as those to whom Peter wrote, that is,
false teachers. No date can be assigned to this
writing with any degree of certainty.

Structure

Introduction (vv. 1-2)
1. A call to contend for the faith (vv. 3-4)
2. Past judgements (vv. 5-7)
3. The false teachers (vv. 8-19)
4. A call to grow in the faith (vv. 20-23)
A closing doxology (vv. 24-25)

Overview

Jude seems to have desired to write his readers
a treatise about the salvation he and his readers

TEACHING

shared, but the threat of false teachers made it necessary for him to deal with that issue. He wrote, then, to
urge his readers to 'contend earnestly for the faith' (v.
3). By 'the faith' he was referring to the body of truth that
had been given once and for all to the people of God.

Those who were attacking this body of truth were
heading for severe judgement. The same God who had
judged rebellious Israelites (v. 5), rebellious angels (v.
6) and Sodom and Gomorrah (v. 7) would also judge
these teachers (vv. 14-15). Jude describes the teachers
as clever and subtle (v. 4), permissive (v. 4), without
respect for authority (vv. 8-10), greedy (v. 11) and arro-
gant and shameless, evidently practising immorality
at the fellowship meal that preceded the observance of
the Lord's Supper (v. 12). Furthermore, they were selfish and thoughtless ('serving only themselves' — v. 12),
spiritually barren and unproductive (v. 13) and under
the condemnation of God (v. 13). They were also grum-
blers (v. 16), lustful (v. 16) and flatterers (v. 16).

The best way for Jude's readers to stand against these
teachers was to do the following:

1. study (v. 20)
2. pray in the Holy Spirit (v. 20)
3. rejoice in salvation (v. 21) — 'keep yourselves in the
   love of God' means they were to walk in the sun-
   shine of God's love, to live each day conscious of
   the fact that God had loved them and saved them
4. look forward to eternal life (v. 21)
5. help others (vv. 22-23)

DISCUSS IT

1. Read Ephesians 4:11-16. What do these verses teach about the matter of Christian growth?

2. Read 2 Corinthians 11:5-15. How does Paul characterize false teachers in this passage?

3. Read 1 Corinthians 16:13; Philippians 1:27; 1 Timothy 3:9; Titus 1:10-14. What do they tell us about 'the faith'?

THE GUIDE

CHAPTER
FIFTY-ONE

THE FIRST, SECOND AND THIRD EPISTLES OF JOHN

BIBLE BOOK

THE FIRST, SECOND AND THIRD EPISTLES OF JOHN

1 JOHN

Introduction

The epistles of John were written by the apostle John. He was one of the original twelve disciples of Jesus, and also wrote the Gospel of John.

John does not identify his readers, but tradition has it that his three epistles were directed to churches in Asia Minor. The three epistles are usually dated some time between A.D. 90 and 100.

Purpose

John's readers, like those to whom the apostle Peter wrote, were facing the heresy of false teachers. These teachers, known as 'Gnostics', claimed to have been given a special anointing or enlightenment (the Greek word '*gnosis*' means 'knowledge').

John wrote to refute these false beliefs and to explain the marks of those who truly know God (5:13).

Structure

1 John does not lend itself to neat analysis as John continually goes back over ground he has already covered. It is obvious that he was not writing an academic treatment to be analysed and outlined by literary people, but as a pastor who was profoundly concerned about his people. He keeps addressing his readers as his 'little children' (2:1,12,13,28; 3:7,18; 4:4; 5:21). He had a tender regard for these people, and, seeing them threatened by false teachers, he poured forth a torrent of words to awaken them.

1. The refutation of errors (1:1 - 2:2)
2. The tests of faith (2:3 - 5:12)
    a. First cycle (2:3-27)
    b. Second cycle (2:28 - 4:6)
    c. Third cycle (4:7 - 5:5)
3. Concluding assurances (5:6-21)

Overview

The refutation of errors (1:1 - 2:2)

There were many different kinds of gnosticism in the early Christian era, but the kind with which John was dealing had these distinguishing marks:

1. a belief that the body is evil and that Jesus could not, therefore, have been God in human flesh

2. a belief that sin does not exist either in our nature or our behaviour, or, if it does, it does not interfere with our fellowship with God

John responds to the first of these by reminding his readers that he had actually seen with his eyes and handled with his hands the Lord Jesus Christ, and his flesh was real (1:1).

He responds to the second error by insisting that sin does indeed interfere with our fellowship with God (1:5-7) and that it resides in our nature (1:8-10). With each of these affirmations, John includes assurances of God's readiness to forgive (1:7; 2:1-2).

The tests of faith (2:3 - 5:12)

John devoted the major part of his letter to elaborating three marks of true faith in Christ. These marks or tests are as follows:

1. the test of belief
2. the test of obedience
3. the test of love

These three marks are presented in three cycles:

1. *First cycle* (2:3-27)
   obedience (2:3-6)
   love (2:7-11)
   belief (2:18-27)

2. *Second cycle* (2:28 - 4:6)
   obedience (2:28 - 3:10)
   love (3:11-18)
   belief (4:1-6)

3. *Third cycle* (4:7 - 5:5)
   love (4:7-12)
   belief (4:13-21)
   obedience (4:21 – 5:5)

A summary of the three tests is presented in the opening verses of chapter five (vv. 1-5).

Concluding assurances (5:6-21)

John brings his epistle to a close by giving three witnesses to Christ and the consequent assurance his readers could have regarding salvation and prayer. The three witnesses are as follows:

1. *the water* — a reference to Jesus' baptism upon which the Father spoke from heaven to attest that Jesus was indeed his Son
2. *the blood* — a reference to Jesus' death on the cross. On the Mount of Transfiguration, Jesus spoke with Moses and Elijah about his death, and the Father again spoke from heaven to attest that Jesus was his Son
3. *the Holy Spirit* — who came for the express purpose of bearing witness to Jesus as the Son of God

2 AND 3 JOHN

These short letters are very similar. One point of similarity is that the author simply identifies himself as 'the elder' in both letters. The style of writing in each leaves no doubt that John was the author.

In both letters John expresses his desire to visit. In both letters he instructs his readers to welcome travelling teachers and preachers. Still another point of similarity is that both letters have the same general theme: walking in the truth.

There are also, of course, differences between the letters. 2 John was addressed to 'the elect lady and her children', which was probably the apostle's way of referring to a church. 3 John, on the other hand, was written to an individual. We might say, then, that 2 John was written to commend a church for walking in the truth, and 3 John was written to commend an individual for walking in the truth.

Some of the key points we glean from 2 John are as follows:

1. walking in the truth should be our supreme priority (v. 4)
2. walking in the truth requires us to love one another (vv. 5-6)
3. walking in the truth requires caution and watchfulness (vv. 7-9)

TEACHING

3 John commends a man named Gaius for walking in the truth. It consists primarily of the following:

1. *a prayer* (vv. 2-4). The apostle prays that Gaius' prosperity in every area of life will be in direct proportion to his spiritual prosperity. A daring prayer!

2. *a proof* (vv. 5-8). One of the evidences that Gaius was indeed walking in the truth was the hospitality he had shown to travelling ministers. John notes that while godly preachers and teachers were to be treated warmly by God's people, false teachers were to be firmly rejected.

3. *a warning* (vv. 9-10). The apostle cautions Gaius to be on guard against Diotrephes, who loved to have pre-eminence and who had spoken maliciously of John.

3 John presents us with three men: Gaius, Diotrephes and Demetrius, who had 'a good testimony' (v. 12). The first and last serve as positive examples for us to follow.

QUESTIONS FOR DISCUSSION

1. *Read John 13:34-35. What results from Christians loving each other?*

2. Are Christians responsible for obeying God's commands? Where are his commands found? With what spirit are we to obey them? Read John 14:15,21; Romans 6:17; 2 Timothy 3:16-17; James 1:22-27.

CHAPTER
FIFTY-TWO

THE
REVELATION OF
JESUS CHRIST

BIBLE BOOK

THE REVELATION OF JESUS CHRIST

Introduction

The book of Revelation was written by an imprisoned apostle to persecuted churches.[1] While the apostle John penned this letter from his exile on the Isle of Patmos, it was and is the revelation of the Lord Jesus Christ himself (1:1).

A date of A.D. 95 is favoured by many for this book. This would place John's writing of it during the severe persecution of Christians under the reign of the Roman emperor Domitian.

Purpose and theme

One could easily get the impression these days that the purpose of Revelation was to give believers a very complex prophetic riddle to solve. Actually it was given to encourage the churches to which it was addressed. The theme of the book is the complete and final victory of the Lord Jesus Christ and his church over Satan and his various agents.

Schools of interpretation

1. The Futurist school regards most of the book to be a depiction of events that are yet to come.
2. The Preterist view sees Revelation as a highly symbolic description of events that surrounded the fall of Jerusalem in A.D. 70.
3. The Historicist position maintains that the book was intended to give its readers insight into the period of time from Christ's first coming to his second coming.
4. The Idealist school suggests the book was designed to give, not specific events, but rather certain principles of spiritual warfare that are applicable to every generation of Christians.

Some insist that it is not necessary to choose one of these schools to the exclusion of all the others, that a view that embodies the general tenets of each school is best. These four schools constitute general interpretative approaches to Revelation. The following are schools of thought regarding the thousand-year millennial period mentioned in Revelation 20:1-10.

1. *Premillenialists* believe the thousand-year period is to be understood literally, and is a time when Christ will rule and reign over the earth after he comes in great power and glory. This will be a time of perfect peace and harmony because Satan will be bound. After the millennium Satan will be loosed and will once again

deceive the nations, before he is finally cast into the lake of fire. It will be after this period that the eternal state begins.

2. *Amillenialists* maintain that there will be no literal thousand-year millennial reign, that this is rather a symbol for the present gospel age. They believe Satan is, in a sense, bound now through the preaching of the gospel.

3. *Postmillenialists* believe the thousand-year period precedes the coming of Christ. They argue that the kingdom will experience great expansion and growth through the preaching of the gospel until it finally enjoys universal triumph. At that point Christ will return.

Structure

Revelation consists of four great visions, each of which includes the phrase 'in the Spirit' (1:9; 4:2; 17:3; 21:10).

Introduction (1:1-8)
1. First vision: Christ and the church (1:9 - 3:22)
2. Second vision: Christ and the world (4:1 - 16:21)
   a. The seven seals (4:1 - 8:1)
   b. The seven trumpets (8:2 - 11:19)

Overview

Introduction (1:1-8)

John here states that he was about to share 'The Revelation of Jesus Christ' about 'things which must shortly take place' (1:1) with the seven churches of Asia (1:4). He immediately states his major theme: God will eventually vindicate the crucified Christ (1:7-8).

First vision: Christ and the church (1:9 - 3:22)

In this vision John sees the glorified and majestic Christ (1:9-17) and receives from him letters to send to seven churches. Each of these churches had a distinct feature or characteristic:

1. Ephesus — lost first love (2:1-7)
2. Smyrna — persecuted (2:8-11)
3. Pergamos — doctrinal falsehood (2:12-17)
4. Thyatira — lack of holiness (2:18-29)
5. Sardis — deadness (3:1-6)
6. Philadelphia — faithfulness (3:7-13)
7. Laodicea — lukewarmness (3:14-22)

Second vision: Christ and the world (4:1 - 16:21)

This vision consists primarily of four series of sevens: the seven seals (4:1 - 8:1), the seven trumpets (8:2 - 11:19), the seven signs (12:1 - 14:20) and the seven bowls (15:1 - 16:21).

1. The seven seals represent the world's persecution of the church.
2. The seven trumpets represent the initial judgements of God upon the world for persecuting his people.
3. The seven signs (the woman, the dragon, the Man-Child, the archangel Michael, the beast from the sea, the beast from the earth, and the Lamb on Mount Zion) picture the world's conflict with the church on a deeper level. The dragon (Satan) employs the beast from the sea (persecuting government), the beast from the earth (false religion), and Babylon (the seductiveness of the world). These three allies of Satan centre their attack, respectively, on the bodies, minds and hearts of believers.
4. The seven bowls represent God's final wrath upon impenitent persecutors.

Third vision: Christ and victory (17:1 - 20:15)

In this vision John sees the two beasts and Babylon defeated and Satan himself is 'cast into the lake of fire and brimstone' (20:10).

John also sees the Great White Throne Judgement (20:11-15), in which all 'the dead, small and great' stand before God. Anyone whose name was 'not found written in the Book of Life was cast into the lake of fire' (20:15).

Fourth vision: Christ and eternity (21:1 - 22:5)

John is given a detailed vision of the heavenly city 'coming down out of heaven from God' (21:2). Many have a mistaken notion of what the eternal state will be like for believers. They see the saints as spirits floating around in a heaven that is up in the clouds. John's vision shows us that the eternal state is this: saints in glorified bodies will inhabit a new city that has come down to a new earth. This will be a place where there is no sorrow, pain or death (21:4).

Conclusion (22:6-21)

The apostle closes this book by exhorting his readers to obey the commandments of the Lord (22:7,14-15) and by warning them not to add to or take from this prophecy (22:18-19).

QUESTIONS FOR DISCUSSION

1. *Read Psalm 45:13-17; 110:1; Daniel 2:44; 7:13-14; Micah 4:1-13; Habakkuk 2:14; 1 Corinthians 15:24-28;*

Philippians 2:5-11. What do these verses tell us about the Lord Jesus Christ and his kingdom? Does the book of Revelation give us the fulfilment of these promises?

2. *Read Romans 8:18-25. What is the future of this earth?*

NOTES

Chapter 2
1. *The Open Bible: The New King James Version*, Thomas Nelson Publishers, p.1.

Chapter 6
1. Warren Wiersbe, *With the Word*, Oliver Nelson, p.125.

Chapter 8
1. *The Open Bible*, p.236.

Chapter 11
1. S. G. DeGraaf, *Promise and Deliverance*, Presbyterian and Reformed, vol. ii, p.200.

Chapter 12
1. J. Sidlow Baxter, *Explore the Book*, Zondervan Publishing House, p.118.

Chapter 16
1. David Atkinson, *The Bible Speaks Today: The Message of Job*, Inter-Varsity Press, p.57.
2. *MacArthur Study Bible: New King James Version*, Word Bibles, p.694.

Chapter 17
1. John R.W. Stott, *Favorite Psalms*, Moody Press, p.5.
2. Henrietta C. Mears, *What the Bible Is All About*, Regal Books, p.183.
3. *The Open Bible*, p.539.
4. As above, p.538.

Chapter 18
1. William Hendriksen, *Survey of the Bible*, Baker Book House, p.283.
2. Baxter, *Explore the Book*, p.132.

Chapter 19
1. Stuart Olyott, *A Life Worth Living and a Lord Worth Loving*, Evangelical Press, Introduction.
2. Wiersbe, *With the Word*, p.436.
3. Irving L. Jensen, *Jensen's Survey of the Old Testament*, Moody Press, p.301.
4. Olyott, *A Life Worth Living*, pp.75-6.

Chapter 20
1. *The Open Bible*, p.676.

Chapter 21
1. *The Open Bible*, pp.741-2.

Chapter 22
1. Jensen, *Jensen's Survey,* p. 364.
2. As above, p.366.
3. *New Geneva Study Bible*, p.1257.
4. *The Open Bible*, p.812.

Chapter 23
1. Stuart Olyott, *Dare to Stand Alone*, Evangelical Press, p.86.

Chapter 25
1. *The New Bible Dictionary*, William B. Eerdmans Publishing Co., p.639.
2. *Holman Bible Dictionary*, Holman Bible Publishers, p.341.
3. J. I. Packer, *God Speaks to Man*, Westminster Press, p.9.

NOTES

Chapter 26
1. *New Geneva Study Bible*, p.1412.
2. O. Palmer Robertson, *Jonah: A Study in Compassion*, Banner of Truth Trust, p.16.

Chapter 29
1. *New Geneva Study Bible: New King James Version*, Thomas Nelson Publishers, p.1461.
2. Jensen, *Jensen's Survey*, pp.463-4.
3. As above, p.464.

Chapter 30
1. T. Miles Bennett, *The Broadman Bible Commentary: Malachi*, Broadman Press, vol. vii, p.368.
2. Joyce G. Baldwin, *Tyndale Old Testament Commentaries: Haggai, Zechariah, Malachi*, Inter-Varsity Press, p.211.

Chapter 35
1. *MacArthur Study Bible*, p.1630.

Chapter 36
1. Donald Grey Barnhouse, *Romans*, Wm. B. Eerdmans Publishing Company, vol. i, p.2.
2. As above.
3. *Holman Bible Dictionary*, p.1204.
4. *The Open Bible*, p.1140.

Chapter 37
1. Leon Morris, *The First Epistle of Paul to the Corinthians*, Wm. B. Eerdmans Publishing Company, p.86.

Chapter 39
1. *NAC News: Newsletter about the New American Commentary*, vol. i, no.6, p.1.
2. As above.

3. John R.W. Stott, *Only One Way: The Message of Galatians*, Inter-Varsity Press, p.36.

Chapter 42
1. Geoffrey B. Wilson, *Colossians and Philemon*, Banner of Truth Trust, p.11.
2. Curtis Vaughn, *Colossians: A Study Guide*, Zondervan Publishing House, p.90.

Chapter 43
1. *The Open Bible*, p.1220.

Chapter 46
1. Geoffrey B. Wilson, *The Pastoral Epistles*, Banner of Truth Trust, p.117.
2. *MacArthur Study Bible*, pp.1890-91.

Chapter 52
1. *The Celebrate Jesus! Millennium Bible*, Holman Bible Publishers, p.1607.

NOTES